GIG OUT

The ULTIMATE GUIDE

To

Finding Your Side Hustle in the Gig Economy

(with about 100 great ideas for easy side gigs you can start today)

Dana Robinson

Forward by Jim Wang, CEO WalletHacks.com

Published by Opt Out Media, San Diego, California. OptOut.media

OPT OUT is a trademark of Opt Out Media.

Printed in the United States of America.

10 9 8 7 6 5 4 3 2 1

ISBN: 978-1-7322872-2-8 (Paperback)

ISBN: 978-1-7322872-3-5 (Kindle)

Cover design by Shena Honey Lagapa Pulido via Yna @ 99designs.com

Layout design by Fiverr

Author Photo by Flavio Scorsato, flaviophotography.com

rendering legal, accounting, or other professional services herein. If you need legal, accounting or other professional advice, you must seek your own professional and not look to this book as a substitute for such services. Some stories and names have been intentionally changed to preserve privacy and some creative liberties are taken in the interest of efficiency, but are immaterial in the opinion of the author.

Dana Robinson is a licensed attorney in California and Nevada, and a licensed real estate broker in California. However, his writing in this and other books and in other media is not intended as legal or real estate advice. Such advice should be specifically tailored to suit your needs. Books that provide self-help, including this one, are not a replacement or substitute for professional advice, which must be given considering your specific needs.

Join the OPT OUT LIFE tribe at www.optoutlife.com where Dana and his business partner Nathaniel Broughton share their experiences and interview successful entrepreneurs, creatives, world travelers, and people applying life-hacking skills that provide freedom and lifestyle. Find their podcast, Opt Out Life, wherever podcasts are available, including the Apple Store.

Table of Contents

Dedication

This book is dedicated to Cory Verner, not only as a friend and business partner, but as a member of the millions of side gig hustlers who mowed lawns, painted houses in college, and have spent their lives hustling opportunities and working to build a life they control.

Foreword

When I first met Dana, I was surprised to learn that he practiced law. I'd always thought lawyers were diligently uptight rule followers who were always wearing bespoke suits with fancy white shoes.

This did not describe Dana.

That's not to say I didn't believe it. Dana was calm, always analyzing the situation, and seemed to be able to distill it down to its most important ideas. Valuable skills in law, even more valuable in life.

We'd spent time together socially and I never learned his entire story until I read it in his first book, Opt Out. I'd heard bits and pieces, like his time in Bali, but to read it in a single narrative was a treat and almost a second education in how life really worked.

My big takeaway from his first book was that you don't have to live the life you thought you were supposed to. You don't have to work that 9-to-5 job you hate. You don't have to obediently follow society's idea of what you should do next – buy a house, buy an expensive car, get married, and then work to support it until you couldn't.

There are many ways to live your life and I can't think of anyone better to show you than someone who has done it himself.

As for me, I stumbled onto a similar revelation by accident

It was 2005 and I was working as a software engineer at a large defense contractor. It was a good job that paid well but was unremarkable. It was the kind of job your parents would be proud of. The kind of thing college counselors tell you to do. But, it wasn't giving me the life I dreamed of.

Having a vanilla job gave me a lot of free time, so I thought it would be fun to start a blog about personal finance called Bargaineering. Back then, a blog was seen more like a personal journal than a money-making venture. I remember telling my girlfriend that it would be great if the blog could make enough to pay for one vacation a year – that's all I expected from it!

And that's the beauty of a side gig – it starts small and, sometimes it has the potential to grow into something bigger. For years, it didn't make more than a few hundred dollars a month. That's not a lot of money compared to a typical job but it's a tremendous amount when you consider it "extra" money. And that "extra" money gives you financial flexibility. It gives you the freedom to make better decisions about your life and your work from a position of strength.

I saved up some of that extra money and invested it in the stock market. I used that money as a cushion and quit my job. It gave me the confidence to choose to make my side hustle my main hustle. Those savings could support me for over a year even if my blog's income dropped to zero. And with additional time each day to work on my "side" project, the site blossomed.

The site didn't grow out of luck or an accident – it was the product of my extra time and attention. It was also a result of the seeds I had planted when I had a day job, slowly and diligently adding content when I had a stable income from my W2 job. Once I took the leap, I was able to test out ideas, make small and large bets, and learn more about how to succeed in the business because I had more time to devote to it. I could afford to make mistakes because my time wasn't as precious and some of those decisions became home runs.

Once I owned my time, I could invest in my own education about internet marketing and about SEO. I could hire freelance writers to help me create content for the site. The side hustle grew to become a legit business even though there was only one full-time employee – me. Not all side hustles grow like this but when they do, it's magical.

With the income and free time, I could also go to conferences where I met other people and grew my network, adding to my quiver of resources that continued to help me grow my business. It was in this capacity that I met Nate Broughton, Dana's partner in crime at the Opt Out Life, at a conference of internet entrepreneurs. It was through Nate that I would meet Dana, of whom Nate often spoke reverently about. It was only then that I realized how many people were choosing to live life outside of the traditional path.

Whether these are expats working remotely from an exotic beach location to driving part-time for a ridesharing platform, the idea that your 9-to-5 is your only source of income bordered on reckless.

Your full-time job is important, but you need to work on outside projects because those projects are 100% yours. You don't do them because your boss tells you. The company doesn't own your creations.

You get to learn a tremendous amount about the work but also yourself. You get to keep what you build; you get to keep what you earn, and all the decisions are yours – for better or for worse. Also, they have the potential to grow much bigger and much faster than you expect – with you keeping all the upside.

And that's what happened to me - the blog earnings grew to the point that I quit my job as a software engineer to pursue it full-time. The side gig, which never aspired to become a business, had outgrown the side gig moniker and was something I had to devote all my time. A few years later, I would sell that little blog for seven figures to a publicly traded company, Bankrate – a result I could never have imagined. Let this sink in. I didn't go raise money and launch a startup. I didn't have a genius idea, a patent, or an unique acumen in the space I entered. I just started doing something and kept on doing it until the revenue grew. And, I took the "big exit" that every starry-eyed startup entrepreneur dreams of.

And the best part is that after my noncompete expired, I started another personal finance blog at WalletHacks.com that is even more successful than my first. I took all the lessons I learned from the first blog and rolled it into the second. That's the beauty of side hustles, the skills you learn translate to a variety of situations.

I was very lucky to have stumbled into these lessons because these are not the lessons you learn in school. These are also not "hard" to implement but it's easy to go down rabbit holes and waste years pursuing the wrong thing.

There's also the issue of not knowing what you don't know. If you've only known of one path in life, learning that there **is** no path can be scary. It helps to learn from others, through their own experiences.

If this describes you, I am here to assure you that you made a good choice in getting this book. Everyone needs a side hustle. It doesn't have to be something that becomes a business. It doesn't have to be more than a little extra income. But we all need a hustle that we can nurture and care for.

This book will provide a powerful framework for how to build your own side gig lifestyle wrapped in rich stories about others who have done the same.

You will be educated, you'll be inspired, and you'll have a good time – just be ready to do the work when you're done!

-Jim Wang, CEO

WalletHacks.com

About Jim Wang

Jim Wang has been writing about personal finance for over 15 years and been featured in the New York Times, Baltimore Sun, Marketplace Money, Entrepreneur, BusinessWeek, U.S. News and World Report, and more.

He's also written for The Vanguard Group, Intuit's TurboTax, Ally Bank, Forbes, and more.

Jim didn't learn about money in the classroom (heck, no one did). He didn't get a certification and he's not an adviser or coach. He learned about building wealth through trial and error. He learned by doing it. And, he built a blog to help others do it. He sold that blog for $3 million, which empowered himself to live the life he wanted. He's spent the past decade doing it again: building ***Best Wallet Hacks*** beyond even his earlier success.

Jim subscribes to the importance of having a side hustle to achieve financial success. He lives in Maryland with his lovely wife and four children.

Introduction

There are hundreds of books about how to start a business, how to get a business up and running, and how to run a business better.

This book isn't one of them. Instead, this book is about how ***not*** to own a business.

Why would I write an entire book about how *not* to own a business?

Because you don't need a business. Businesses have risk. Businesses require major capital.

What you need is a *non-business*.

What you need is a ***side gig.***

What is a side gig? A side gig is something you can do with very little time that makes a steady stream of money, month after month.

A side gig does not require a large up-front or ongoing investment. A side gig does not have high risk. It is designed to be low-stress.

Sounds perfect, right? You'll see dozens of different side gigs throughout this book. My own side gigs have included informational websites, a plant nursery, an import/export business, real estate brokering, and many others.

You may have noticed how many people are driving Uber or Lyft on the weekends. You may have been getting a haircut and had your barber tell you that he's also running a social media agency, or you may have met a bartender who is also launching a web startup.

Side gigs abound, and the number of people doing side gigs is growing rapidly. In fact, side gigs are changing the American economy for the first time since prior to the Industrial Revolution.

Here's a fun experiment to prove my point: Start asking people what their side gig is before they've even said they have one! You'll be surprised at how many people readily answer the question…because the fact is that more and more people have a side gig.

According to economist Arun Sundararajan, America's founding fathers described a "genuine market economy" with individuals engaging in commerce with each other.

America was originally a gig economy. And we are headed there again. It presents the opportunity of a lifetime for those willing to seize it.

Today we have a massive rise in the number of individuals who perform "gigs" rather than go to traditional jobs, or who are doing gigs *and* going to work. Much of this new gig economy is being driven by massive platforms that provide a low barrier to entry for those who want to generate money from a side gig. These platforms allow millions of sellers and buyers to interact and conduct transactions.

AirBnB, VRBO, and HomeAway let you rent your room, apartment or condo by matching you with potential renters. Uber and Lyft let you work as a freelance driver by matching you with consumers who need rides. Piggyback lets you do the same with packages rather than people. Luxe matches you to a valet to park your car when you can't figure out where to park in a big city like New York or San Francisco.

And the list goes on…

BlaBlaCar lets you share your commute. Instacart lets you shop for someone who needs groceries bought and delivered. Drizzly does the same for booze. TaskRabbit lets you do the same with all sorts of tasks, including shopping. Fiverr lets you sell your gig to millions of potential buyers. Etsy lets you sell your handmade items to millions of customers.

You can rent your own car to people through Turo, Getaround and others, depending on where you live. You can teach and earn money through Skillshare, Udemy and Coursera. 99Designs lets you sell your design skill, while Upwork and Field Nation let you sell your skill for any virtual task. Handy matches cleaning staff to cleaning jobs. Other platforms abound.

And let's not ignore platforms that have existed for more than a decade, empowering people to run their gigs efficiently. Craigslist, YouTube, eBay, Etsy, and Alibaba and other websites let consumers sell products quickly and easily into an eager, massive marketplace.

We call this *the crowd economy*, the collaborative economy, the blue economy, the sharing economy, and the peer economy. One website lists more than thirty phrases used to describe the "new" gig economy.

So, what's *new* about it? Well, from the time of industrialization until recently, the American workforce was mostly consolidated into buildings, worked in a hierarchy with defined structure, and worked for companies within the confines of a set schedule to receive a steady paycheck. We went from a gig economy in John Adam's day to post-industrial mass employment in the 20th Century. Now we're moving into a new era in which individuals act as egalitarian market actors with individual power to negotiate and sell their goods or services.

One well-known side-gigger Dan Schawbel started a side gig while working a day job, and then used that to incubate another side gig, and has perpetuated his gig-to-gig lifestyle ever since.

One of Schawbel's businesses has dug deep into the gig culture. Not only does he make a living with side gigs, he has marshalled side gig data that he uses for marketing his businesses.

According to Schawbel's millennialbrand.com:

- 72% of those still at "regular" jobs want to quit to be entirely independent; 61% say they likely will within two years.
- Freedom is the top reason those at "regular" jobs would like to quit; and 89% say they prefer to work when and where they choose (versus in a corporate, 9-to-5 job).
- 90% of independent workers indicated that being an entrepreneur reflects having a certain mindset (rather than being strictly defined as having started a company).
- 58% of freelancing millennials consider themselves "entrepreneurs."

The survey focused on millennials, that population born between the early '80s and 2000, and who account for more than 75 million of the estimated 330 million Americans.

While many herald the gig economy as a good thing, some warn that it will allow large companies to exploit workers.

Predictably, litigation has ensued. For example, Uber, the ride-sharing platform, has been sued for failing to treat its contractors as employees.

However, you must remember that the giant platforms such as Uber are not the only way to score a side gig. The gig platforms are evidence of the cultural shift from traditional employment to gig employment.

Yes, these big platforms are a great way to start something with low risk and no capital. But their size and profit motive can lead them to fostering exploitative conditions, meaning they're not necessarily the Holy Grail of self-employment, either.

But here's the thing. Even if a giant category such as ride sharing creates behemoth companies that become exploitative, there is a low enough barrier to entry that other platforms can enter and compete. An Uber driver can leave Uber and drive for Lyft, for example, or one of many other driving services. Likewise, someone making money on a freelancing platform such as Upwork can always "flip the bird" to the platform and go solo once they prove themselves to their clients.

The American workforce is more educated than ever. You don't need to be bound by corporate structures when there are so many opportunities to get out and make money in the gig economy. The gig economy does not diminish people's freedom or income; it increases both.

The new era for workers did not begin with the gig platforms. It began when the internet made it easy for a person to sell their goods or services on the web. For example, as a young lawyer I was able to leave a large law firm and start my own practice. Prior to the advent of email and web-based services, it was very costly to operate a law firm. When I left to go solo in 2004, I did not need a paralegal because most of my work was done online; corporate filings, trademarks, and even client communication shifted from cumbersome paper-and-mail, to email and digital communication.

The internet didn't just level the legal playing field—thousands of other jobs went digital, too. This freed us from the need to hitch our wagon to the corporate engine. The gig economy is a natural outgrowth of the freelance economy that already started more than 15 years ago. It isn't going away, and regulating the sharing platforms won't stop it, either.

The point of this book is not to simply list the sharing platforms where you might find a gig. You can use your favorite search engine to find those. The focus of this book is to give you real stories of real side gigs that will give you real ideas that are even better than what you'll find on a gig platform. Most of the things you can do for a side gig are not found on gig platforms. The ultimate side gig will be something you do without having to connect to a platform. Instead, platforms will serve as a bridge that allows you to take the leap from working for a company to working for yourself.

What does it mean to have a side gig?

Well, let's start with the money. A side gig means extra cash every month. Even an extra $400 per month would make a huge difference in the daily lives of most Americans. And make no mistake: You can do much better than $400 per month. What if you made $1,000, or even $4,000 per month? And what if it took only a few hours to maintain that income?

Wait — earning thousands of dollars per month without working more than a few hours per week? Sounds crazy, right?

This is the dream repeatedly sold by multi-level marketers and infomercials. There's a reason this dream is sold to us continually through classified ads, windshield flyers, email blasts, or through your cousin Frank who wants to talk to you about his "amazing" product that just so happens to come with a "ground floor opportunity."

It's because the notion of relatively simple and low-effort monthly income is, in fact, the undying dream of millions of Americans.

There's just one problem: Most people selling this particular dream aren't achieving it for themselves.

I'd like to help you achieve that dream. But it doesn't come from infomercial products, or selling multi-level-marketing products (Amway, Tupperware, Avon, Arbonne, Herbalife, etc.) to your friends and family.

The financial freedom you want comes from *owning your very own side gig*.

Back to the money. What is the significance of an extra $400 per month? If you are 35 years old, and save just $400 per month, this should grow to nearly $1 million by the time you are 70 years old. If you have a day job and a growing retirement account already, then you can imagine how an *additional* million dollars will make your later years even more awesome. If you are already at retirement age and living on a small pension and Social Security, then $400 per month may mean the difference between living well, or never having enough. Of course, if your side gig makes even *more* than $400 per month, well, then the impact on your life will be even greater.

What will you do with that additional $400 per month? It's your choice, of course! You might choose to save it, you may want to travel, buy a nice car or live in a better house. If you're already happy with your life and income, and your retirement is growing without any extra help, then you could use your newfound income to pay down your house, help your family, pay for your kid's college, or any number of things.

Most side gigs will make more than $400 per month. My side gigs make thousands. In this book you'll see many examples of attainable side gigs in which $400 monthly is on the low end; most make well over $1,000 per month.

Let me be clear about something. This is a business book about "non-businesses." These side gigs aren't *businesses*.

So what if you want a "real" business? Well, you can have both! In fact, it's a good idea to have a side gig if you eventually want to own a "real" business, too. Starting a real business has risks, and requires that you invest capital, as well as your time, without getting anything back for what could be a long while. Because businesses need cash up front, and you need cash-flow in order to survive the early startup phase, what you need *before* you start a business is a side gig.

Wait. Am I saying you should have a business *and* a non-business?

Short answer: Yes.

Longer answer: I advise aspiring entrepreneurs to have both a "real" business *and* a side gig. However, if you are happy and doing well as an employee, then maybe you just need to keep your day job and start a side gig for extra cash.

There's no need to start a "real" business if you already have an awesome job, a great life and are making the money you want. If that's you, then a side gig just might be the perfect icing on your financial cake. No need to own a business as well.

Why do I advise budding entrepreneurs to own a business *and* a side gig?

Well, for starters, most new entrepreneurs do not have the required cash to start a real business. And a side gig produces income that will help you launch that new business when you're ready. This helps you avoid the pitfalls of trying to raise capital through investors. Unless you are a seasoned business owner, I advise against trying to raise money from investors.

Let me explain. You've probably seen *Shark Tank*, the popular TV show in which entrepreneurs pitch their ideas to the "sharks," who are investors willing to buy into the venture.

Let's forget about the fact that your chances of becoming a contestant on the TV show itself are almost nil. What about the general strategy? Can you raise working capital for your startup from investors this way? Absolutely. However, your odds are slim and it's generally not wise to do so. Fewer than 1 percent of companies vying for venture capital actually get funded. Moreover, even if you do raise money (from friends or family, for example), you will no longer completely own your venture, you will have duties to your investors, and if your venture fails you'll ruin your relationships with those investors. It's far better to save those relationships and potential investors for a later venture, or for when your business has reached a certain level of success and your risk of failure has diminished.

Bottom line: avoid investors. Your business should be funded by you and you alone.

But how can you do that when you have no money? Own a side gig, that's how! Your side gig can fund the launch of your own business, just like it did for New York Times bestselling author Dan Schawbel, who used funds from his side gig to incubate his business. Or follow Susan Tynan, who worked at the online marketplace LivingSocial and came to discover that customers were not happy with local picture framing services.

Susan worked a side gig at Taxi Magic (now Curb) while she launched her framing company, Framebridge, which went on to have 75 employees by 2015. Both her driving gig and her business were side gigs, with Framebridge eventually turning into a real business.

But here's the key takeaway: That side gig *facilitated* her ability to turn her other endeavor into a full-time business.

My buddy Aaron is an aspiring photographer who creates beautiful photos on massive metal sheets. While his business incubates, he makes money from a grooming and doggy dental business.

Can your side gig become a full-time business? Of course! Your side gig could very well turn into a business. However, it doesn't *have* to blossom into a business to be considered a success. I'll show you some examples in this book of side gigs that should actually *not* become businesses.

But you should know that many amazing companies were started as a side gig. Kim Lavine, for example, went from making microwaveable pillows in her kitchen, to then selling them in kiosks, and then eventually to selling to Saks Fifth Avenue, Macy's, Bed Bath & Beyond and running a company with over $1 million in revenue.

Twitter, Papa John's, Yankee Candle, Gibson Guitar and Craigslist all started as side gigs.

A side gig can fund the launch of a company or it can become a big company in its own right. However, don't get distracted by that tantalizing possibility. If it's meant to be, it will come in due time. To start, let's focus on getting you a side gig that's just a side gig.

The Side Gig Life

I've owned several "full" businesses, and I can tell you that being an entrepreneur is a wonderful experience. Starting a company, growing it, and then selling it is one of the greatest feelings you can have. But I can also tell you that I've worked 12 to 14-hour days every day for years in order to grow a business. While this kind of hard work can have a big payoff, it can also lead to a miserable life that causes family strife, ends friendships and worse. The odds of success are low, and the costs are high. What happens when you work 14-hour days for a year and then your venture fails? Because many entrepreneurs don't plan for the possibility of failure—pouring all of their money, energy and time into their venture—it can be devastating. They bet the farm. They bet their marriage. They bet their happiness.

I'd like to suggest something different.

For most people who are self-employed, I think it's far better off to go after a side gig than to launch a startup.

Startup life is stressful. The odds of success are low, the financial cost is high, raising capital is difficult, and you can burn through a ton of resources and personnel before you even raise any money. An even more important reason to forgo a business for a side gig is this: your personal well-being. Think about it: If you want to start a business, your goal is to become financially independent, right? And financial independence means you can buy yourself the freedom to do what you want, whenever you want, and however you want to do it. And yes, owning a company can get you that life. But it can also lead to being overworked, emotionally spent, and not having the freedom you sought in the first place.

What you get from a side gig is a better life. You get freedom, and you get it without the risks and investment required for a "real" business. When I owned a business, I had to show up and work every day, then work every night, and then get up and do it all over again.

It wasn't until I owned side gigs that I got the life I wanted. I got financially independent, too.

So, what *is* financial independence? It's a phrase that's thrown around a lot, and you'll see what financial independence means to many other people in the stories that follow. But I'll start with my own story.

As I sit writing this book, I am living in Bali, Indonesia. I don't work. When I'm not surfing or exploring, I'm writing books and nurturing my side gigs. I live in a fantastic Balinese villa. I have a full-time housekeeper who cooks, cleans, does the laundry and makes the bed every day. I own a motorbike and can borrow or rent a car inexpensively.

Each month I escape the hustle and bustle of urban Bali and head to a remote island in the Indian Ocean where there are no motorized vehicles, no paved roads, only horse-drawn carts and bicycles. While I'm there, I sip on three-dollar cocktails and dine on fresh caught fish for dinner every night for about five bucks.

Yes, you could say I live like a prince. And the beauty is that to live like this, it costs me less than what my side gigs bring in.

So, how much does it cost for you to live a life like this?

Answer: about $1,000 per month. If you can create a steady side gig making $1,000 per month, then you can probably live in a place like Bali indefinitely and never work again. In other words, a side gig that generates just $1,000 per month might give you the freedom to take a year off, or to take an entire *decade* off. Or to live on an island like I'm doing, or to simply vagabond around the world with a backpack and a laptop. You'll see a story of one such person in this book. For those willing to realign their lives, a side gig can mean total freedom, even if it's just for a limited period of time.

You can live the life of a millionaire without having the millions. In fact, you may have an even *better* life than a millionaire, who likely has to work hard every day to maintain his or her fortune.

You can have the life you want if you have a side gig. You don't need to win the lottery. You don't need to launch a startup and sell it for millions. You don't need to get on *Shark Tank*. You don't need to work long days for years before you can enjoy the good life. You just need a side gig.

What is a side gig? By my definition, a side gig is something that generates regular cash flow without major risks, capital or time. It's something that doesn't require large, up-front capital and doesn't need an ongoing investment of cash. It's something that doesn't cause you to lose sleep or require that you spend a lot of time working on it.

Is this *thing* that I am referring to a unicorn? No. The side gig is real. And believe it or not, side gigs are sitting right under your nose. You just have to learn how to spot them, and then develop a strategy for creating your own.

In this book, I'll show you dozens of amazing side gigs. I'll also give you a variety of suggestions for ways to create your own side gig. I'm not just looking to help you earn an extra few hundred dollars a month. I want to help you find your way up and *out* of the rat race. I want to help you onto the pathway to financial independence.

You may have heard about the book, *The 4-Hour Workweek*. I highly recommend this book, or anything by its author, Tim Ferriss, who sets forth a way to live a footloose life while only working four hours each week. I love his book. I've applied many of Tim's principles to my own life. But with a side gig, you might be able to live a *one-hour* workweek rather than the four-hour workweek! You could choose to live somewhere else, learn to dance, master a new language, become a local in another country. It is all possible once you get your head around the idea of the side gig.

Of course, I'm not here to force *my* view of success on you. If you don't want to travel, or if you don't want to live on a remote island in the Indian Ocean, more power to you. You don't have to use your side gig for *that* life. You might want to simply buy a nice car, golf more, or buy a larger house. You can create whatever life you prefer.

That, to me, is the real meaning of financial independence: the freedom to make decisions with your own time, energy and creativity.

If I can empower you to do that, then I have done my job.

Chapter 1

The Side Hustle

I'd like to tell you about a hustler who started his entrepreneurial career as a kid. When he was ten years old, he would scrape the paint off from pencils and customize them with someone's name for a fee. After his parents divorced, he handed out flyers for $2 per hour in Queens, New York.

As a young adult, he waited tables at Red Lobster. Prompted by his mom, he decided to start his own apparel line. She taught him to sew. When she saw him hustle and sell 80 wool caps for $10 each, she decided to mortgage the house and back him financially. He kept his day job at Red Lobster while he launched what would become the internationally known apparel brand FUBU. Even while FUBU was on the rise, Daymond John kept his Red Lobster job.

Today FUBU has $6 billion per year in global sales, and you've probably seen Daymond as one of the celebrity investors on the television reality show *Shark Tank.*

From the age of 10, Daymond was a hustler in business. If you want to make it in business, you've got to hustle. In fact, a side gig is often called a "side hustle" for this very reason. It's not just a gig. You have to use your head and think outside the box. You've got to hustle. You don't necessarily have to work harder, but you definitely must work smarter. That's what it means to hustle.

I may not be Daymond John, but I learned to hustle when I was young, too. When I was about thirteen, I made hair clips and sold them to girls in my middle school. It was a good way to meet girls, and gave me lunch money so I didn't have to eat warm bologna sandwiches (sorry mom).

I was already an experienced business-kid by then. I had owned the neighborhood lawn business (a veritable cartel under the careful control of my eleven-year-old mind). Before that, I sold trinkets at the swapmeet I had made in the garage; before that, I was a lemonade tycoon.

My mom taught me to sew when I was young. I started making surfboard bags when I was fifteen and sold them to friends and local surf shops. I also worked two part-time jobs. Did I go to school? Of course! I was just a high school kid who also had the entrepreneurial bug. I was learning to hustle.

In college I sold jewelry as a side gig for a little while. I also had a part-time job at Nordstrom selling ties and men's shirts. I also started a landscape maintenance company when I was a sophomore in college.

I've been working a side hustle ever since. And it keeps paying off in wonderful ways. The biggest lesson in hustling is that you often need to get out of your comfort zone and take a crack at something unusual. You need to make a call, or write a letter, or take a shot in the dark.

Let me tell you about how I hustled my way through law school.

When I first decided to go to law school, I was faced with the obvious problem that law school is expensive. I already had a wife and young daughter, and could not envision a way to pay for law school as well as our living expenses. Even with student loans, I would only be able to cover tuition. How could I manage to also pay rent and living expenses, as well as tuition for three years while I obtained my law degree?

At the time, I had a side gig as the apartment manager of a small building. It covered my rent and didn't take much of my time. As a full-time student, I could not have earned that $1,000 per month from part-time work back in 1996. And if I had to work to earn that money, I would have been exhausted. I *needed* a side gig like this.

So how much was this side gig worth? Well, it saved me $36,000 over the course of three years. That's because I would have needed to borrow that same amount in the form of high-interest private student loans. And over the twenty-year life cycle of those loans, the total cost would have been closer to $70,000, which would have burdened my life for two decades.

My apartment manager side gig was not without its downside. I did my share of unclogging toilets, breaking up parties, fixing light switches, and moving furniture. I lost many hours of sleep to noisy tenants. I almost had a fistfight with a huge steroided tenant who insisted his music *wasn't* too loud. I evicted deadbeats. But really, what other side gig could be better for a young law student than one that allowed his family to live on the beach in sunny San Diego? It was awesome.

The beach apartment job was not my only side gig during law school. One side hustle isn't always enough. I did whatever I could to scrounge up some money. One of those hustles was working ten hours per week in the law library computer lab. I literally got paid to sit. Oh sure, I had to unjam the printer sometimes, but for the most part my job was to check IDs to make sure non-law students didn't use our special law library. There was only one catch: During those ten hours, I was not allowed to do any law homework. But I could do just about anything else while I sat in the computer lab.

So here's what I did: I took a part-time job for a legal research service. I also worked as an assistant for a law professor. And I did research for an attorney. I could do these other side gigs while also getting paid to sit in the computer lab.

Even though I had all of those side gigs, I was looking for other hustles. So I started reading about HTML programming at my little desk in the computer lab. I taught myself how to create web pages back in 1997. It seemed like magic.

That led me to NetworkSolutions.com, where I registered a domain name, freelegalaid.com. I was a smart guy, but obviously *not* a genius. Why oh why did I not register money.com, or law.com, or some other awesome one-word domain name back in 1997? Because I'm a benevolent idiot, that's why.

Of all the choices of domain names in 1997, I registered freelegalaid.com. Not a one-word domain name, but a three-word domain. And not a particularly profitable one at that, because consider my domain name — it was designed to provide something for *free*. I'm not always the smartest guy in the room.

Regardless, I went on to build a 2,000-page site that catered to fifty states and forty areas of law. I intended this to be a directory of legal resources; perhaps lawyers would even contribute a little free information for users. It would be good for everyone, and maybe I would make some extra cash as well.

How did this go? Well, I had 10,000 visits per month starting on day one. But at the time, there was no real model for making money from web traffic, so I put the project on the back burner. I would tinker on the weekends and in my free time.

Almost a decade and three iterations later, I finally came up with an online formula that was right for the times. By 2005 I had a homemade site based on PERL (for those who know and care about programming languages), along with a few thousand pages of content I had personally collated.

The site was made $500 per month for several years. That felt like magic. It was my first web-based side gig, and it earned a steady income without any real work on my part. After revamping it yet again, the monthly revenue grew to thousands of dollars per month, and it continues to this day. I mean, I'm in Bali right now living on that money as I type this! And I don't spend even an hour per week working on it.

That website, which was a failure in 1997, now funds my ability to do what I want, where I want. Freelegalaid.com is the quintessential side gig. Do I wish I had registered a better domain like law.com back in 1997, and then sold it for millions? Of course. But I didn't. What I *did* create was a site that has helped hundreds of thousands of people for more than fifteen years and has generated a steady stream of cash I can use to pay my bills while I live in Bali and write books to help people like you. I'd like to think I'm actually better off than if I'd hit it big with a dot-com home run. Remember, what's special about a side gig is that it gives you the lifestyle that most people want, but without the long hours and personal risks and sacrifices.

What makes Freelegalaid.com a great side gig is that it requires no capital, no ongoing investment, very little time, and no stress. It generates a steady monthly income. It's my Bali fund.

Now, you could be excused for wondering, "Hey, if your site is making thousands of dollars each month, can't it make tens of thousands per month, or even hundreds of thousands per month? Couldn't you just take the foundation of freelegalaid.com and build it into something bigger?"

In other words, couldn't I turn this side gig into a "real" business? Yes, I definitely could. But I would need to invest $250,000 in technological redevelopment. I would also need to hire a staff to handle customer service. I would need a marketing person to expand my advertising reach. Another person would need to seek strategic alliances with other legal websites to add content, and to push referrals out to lead generation sites.

In addition to investing $250,000 or more in cash, I would then need to work full-time on that business for a year or two in order to get it up and running as a real business. I would need to ensure that my investors got a return and that the business progressed from its current modest income level to something far greater.

Contrast that to what I have now. All I have to do now is curate content, run some ads and watch the money show up in my bank account each month.

Sure, the potential is there to make big money. But I don't want a side gig that's a business. I want what I call a *non-business*. I simply need the steady cash flow to fund the independent, international life I'm currently living. What this side gig gives me right *now* is the freedom to live in Bali and create more income by writing and publishing. This little side gig is providing me with the life of a millionaire, and I don't have to work hard or put anything at risk in order to have this life. It's the perfect side gig.

Throughout this book you'll see a lot of other examples of side gigs that have varying strengths and weaknesses. Not all of them will be as good as freelegalaid.com, and many will be far better. Some will have the potential to become million dollar businesses, others will not. What you should see at this point is that you can create a side hustle that will change your life forever. It might be the next FUBU, and make you the next billionaire. Or, like my own hustles, your side gig might simply provide a means to pay your way through law school (like my apartment management gig did), or give you a way to vagabond around the world (freelegalaid.com).

Whether your side gig is small or becomes the next "big thing," you have to hustle. You have to stop thinking like everyone else. You can't be shy. You may have to show some gumption and make a phone call, like when I called Tom to ask him if I could manage his apartments. You may have to challenge yourself and learn something new, such as figure out how to code your own web pages. Or you may have to learn to sew wool caps like Daymond John (or surfboard bags like I did).

If you are willing to hustle, then the stories in this book will inspire you. It will set you on a path toward entrepreneurship that, even if it doesn't make you the next Daymond John, can literally transform your life.

Chapter 2

Requirements for a Good Side Gig

Launching a side gig is the functional starting point for getting what I call the Opt Out Life.

That's right, everyone I've interviewed on the Opt Out Life podcast, as well all the examples of the people described in my book, are living the much-coveted Opt Out Life with the help of a side gig.

You don't just *want* a side gig. You ***NEED*** a side gig.

Simply put, the side gig is your most critical tool for opting out of the *"opt in"* life that's been sold to you. You want to live independently on YOUR own terms? Then you need a side gig, period, full stop.

Now before I pass along your first action steps, let's dig into what a side gig is really all about. This is important because you need to understand the proper framework for a side gig.

(Note: This will be easy for those who have read the *Opt Out* book. But for everyone else, pull up a chair because this is where the magic all starts.)

So ... Just what *IS* a side gig?

This is a more layered question than you might think. Not many people step back and ask that question, existentially. Most books about side gigs *praise* them ... or *categorize* them

... or maybe extol their virtues ... but not enough really give you the full picture. This is important stuff with some critical nuances, so let's get going.

The best way to understand a side gig is to describe *what it isn't.*

For starters, **a side gig is NOT a normal business**.

Let us count the ways:

- A normal business has risk and stress. (A side gig is low risk and low stress.)
- A normal business requires a lot of capital, both up front and as you grow. (A side gig does not require much cash to start or maintain.)
- A normal business takes a lot of time. (A side gig should take as little time as possible.)
- A normal business typically has big swings in income. (A side gig reliably chugs along like a champ, depositing regular and potentially ever-increasing sums of cash into your coffers.)

As you can see, side gigs are pretty much the opposite of "normal" businesses. Are you beginning to see why I like side gigs so much?

Side Note: I have a tool I call the Side Gig Calculator that you can use to help you objectively list and evaluate potential side gig ideas. You can sign up for it at www.sidegigcalculator.com

Side Gig FAQ

Question:

Wait a second. Are you saying *not* to own a business? Isn't a side gig a business, too?

Answer:

Yes and no. Side gigs are a *subset of business*. Yes, you do something to make money like any other business would, and sure, some side gigs turn into businesses, and that's fine.

But a true side gig should be treated differently than a full-blown business. We sometimes even refer to a side gig as a "non-business" because you are trying to avoid the typical costs, risks and time required for a "real" business, while still getting the main benefit: *cash flow.*

Remember, the Opt Out Life powers itself from the engine of having money coming in every month that doesn't require much time, stress, or ongoing investment.

Another way to look at it: I want you to have the freedom to quit your job if you want, and that means adding some passive revenue to your monthly income.

Do you want to launch a "REAL" business? Sure, that works, too. Just know that a side gig can provide a financial platform to empower you to do just that.

Side gigs can *teach* you about business, too.

Yup, there's a lot to learn before you own a business. You already know that statistics show that most businesses fail, with the owner losing his or her shirt.

But side gigs have low risk, and don't require much money, which means if they do fail, you simply dust yourself off and start again.

If you've done this a few times, and then finally get a side gig that works, you'll be far more likely to succeed when you put your time and money into a full-blown business venture.

So. Where do we go from here?

Well, because my mission is to help you create your first side gig, I'm going to give you practical pointers so that you can put together your action plan for your very first side gig.

The first step is simply all about getting those creative juices flowing.

So get a legal pad, or open your favorite note-taking app, (or get my Side Gig Calculator) and do the following:

ACTION STEP:

Start brainstorming a list of ideas. Make a list!

Just start writing ideas without regard to practicality or reason.

Begin this today. Begin right now.

Open your mind and think big.

Think broadly. Think out of the box.

Think small, too!

List anything you've dreamed of.

No restrictions. Dumb little ideas. Crazy big ideas. Anything is fine for now.

Don't worry, you'll be crossing stuff off as we go through the book, and hopefully adding new ideas along the way.

Don't focus on the name, brand, or the details of your idea. Don't go checking domain names.

Don't worry about "how." Just list ideas as they come to you.

Take this step seriously! This is important ... and it should be FUN, too.

This idea is to throw lumps of clay on the wheel, and worry about shaping them later. The more lumps of clay the better.

Got it? Great. And realize that making that list is just the beginning. It will become a living, breathing thing. You'll add to your list when an idea hits you. You'll delete items when you realize there are reasons to dump an idea, even one that you loved.

Chapter 3

Microwave Pants & Other Great Ideas

In the last chapter, I laid the foundation of what a side gig is all about, telling you what it is and, more importantly, what it *isn't.* I also sent you off to start brainstorming your own list of side gig ideas.

Got your list? Good, we're about to slay it :-)

In order to prepare you for this list-culling, let's go back to 1982 …

Do you remember the film "Night Shift"? If you want to watch one of Henry Winkler's first roles after "Happy Days" as The Fonz, check it out. It's a gritty comedy, peppered with humor by Michael Keaton, a new employee at a morgue who carries a tape recorder with him so that he can record all of his brainy new ideas.

He's an "*Idea Man.*" And he just *knows* that one of those great ideas is going to hit and make the big time.

His brilliant notions included, um, microwave pants. (You know, because who *doesn't* need slacks that keep you warm *and* can bake a potato while taking your dog for a walk?)

Here's the point: That film character was not alone in buying into the perception that hitting it big requires a totally new idea that no one has ever conceived before.

But here's the reality: *Nothing could be further from the truth.*

In fact, trying to launch a business or side gig around a novel idea is actually the worst idea of them all. Yes, I know, there are plenty of stories — mythological stories involving household names and great innovators — that we hold aloft as inspiration.

But the exception simply proves the rule. I love Napoleon Hill's work, and he tells the story of the inception of Coca Cola in a captivating way.

But I've got news for you: Aspiring to invent the next Coke is going to sideline you from the Opt Out Life. Inventing the next Big Thing doesn't usually make the inventor rich. The patent office is a venerable graveyard of great ideas.

Protecting a cool idea might be worth your money, but it's rarely a good way to launch a side gig. Spending thousands on legal fees is appropriate for a *business* in which you are investing a lot of capital to get the venture off the ground.

But side gigs are different. As I've written earlier, a side gig shouldn't require a lot of up-front investment or legal fees.

The goal with a side gig is to get something that starts making money soon, and not something that takes years and tens of thousands of dollars to get to profitability.

That's right. New ideas aren't good side gigs. They aren't even good businesses.

Okay, sure, if you're a Silicon Valley VC, then go for it. Start the next Facebook, Paypal or Twitter. Good luck to you, and we mean it.

But for the rest of us? We simply want the Opt Out Life.

It's not about great ideas. It's about doing pedestrian things well.

Base hits, not home runs.

Let the titans of tech swing for the fences. They have the money to lose when they don't make it, and they are banking on one grand slam for every hundred losses. You don't have that luxury.

Now let's explain what I mean by "pedestrian." Calling something pedestrian sounds like I'm throwing shade. I'm not. It simply means others are doing it — sometimes many others.

This is not a bad thing. Far from it. Take banks, for example. They open right across the street from other banks. This is because they know something very basic:

Business is about doing something where there's ALREADY a market.

Starbucks knows this. It doesn't hesitate to open near other coffee shops.

And, occasionally, people like my buddy Chuck Patton take a page from that playbook and end up doing just fine ... even across the street from Starbucks! That's right, Chuck started a coffee shop across the street from Starbucks, and killed it.

If you've read *Opt Out*, then you've heard the story of how my buddy Jack and I get together for drinks and spend the evening coming up with novel ideas that will save the world. Jack and I will spitball crazy ideas for fun. And that's just fine. Do the same over wine at your family holiday dinner.

But when it comes to actually implementing a business or side gig, set aside the myth of The Big Idea. Avoid novel ideas like the plague.

So, let's talk about what DOES work for side gig ideas.

Can you guess what the biggest thing to consider is when it comes to any business or side gig?

It's called "the market."

Simply put, the market is the total number of people who are ready, willing and able to buy your product or service. Now to get your product or service *to* the market where it can be seen and noticed ... well, that's where marketing comes in.

You'll deal with that later. For now, you simply must determine whether there even IS a market.

And that gets to the heart of the novelty myth. If you come up with something truly new, then you have to ***create a market***. Do you have any idea what that takes? Millions of dollars. Hundreds of millions in most cases!

We are not the ones creating markets. We achieve the Opt Out Life by ***finding existing markets,*** and then selling to those markets. Simple. But effective. I realize this is something of a buzz-kill. This is the least fun part of the book. But it's time to cross off some really cool ideas on your list.

ACTION STEP NO. 1:

Take any idea on your list that's novel, and cross it out.

Delete it from your worksheet. Delete it from your memory. If there's no existing market, leave it to the big players in the venture capital business to risk their money on it. It's not for you.

If you're not sure whether there's a market, then leave it on your sheet and add a note in the "Market?" column to research it. I want you to prove to yourself that there are others doing it before you decide to spend your time and money pursuing it.

I get it. It's not easy to let your cool ideas go.

You may come back to it over and over. But letting go is important. If you can't let go of a great idea that'll never make money, then you may as well rejoin the rat race and stop chasing the Opt Out Life.

I'm practical. I want to put you in a position of control over your time and money. And to do that, you can't chase myths, dreams and fantasies that will never make money.

ACTION STEP NO. 2:

Can you *add* anything to your list in light of this lesson?

Maybe you now realize that you've seen some good ideas and thought that they were not right for you simply *because* someone else was doing them.

Add those new ideas now! Yep, ideas that you may have thought were "taken" might very well be perfectly good side gigs.

Just because someone has done it previously doesn't mean there's no room for you. In fact, it's probably the exact opposite — it's the literal *validation* of your idea.

Let me give you a quick, helpful story to illustrate this. I can remember when I bought a property management company that my wife ran. We offered the same services as a dozen other companies. We just did it better. And we did quite well with it.

But wait till you hear what happened next ...

A guy entered our market and took a couple of our clients. I saw that he also took my idea of putting flier boxes around the beach community to promote his business.

He actually *did it better than we did.*

Then I saw his website and read his terms and conditions. They were mine, *verbatim!*

Yup ... he had just literally copied me ... and had done it better. His website was a bit better. His branding, marketing and client acquisition were all just doing the same thing as us — but just a little bit better.

A decade later, he's still doing great. He didn't need a novel idea. He just needed to do what others did, but do it better.

As you can tell from my tone, I wasn't offended or outraged. I admired it, in a way.

There's nothing new under the sun, as they say. Find something that works, and just do it better.

ACTION STEP NO. 3:

Add some "boring, pedestrian" ideas to your side gig list that you may have dismissed, but are actually sound ideas that could work for you. Sure, some of these ideas might get nixed later, but for now just consider them as clay added to the wheel.

Chapter 4

Jim's Private Label Glue

Jim Johnson is a serial entrepreneur. He's been in and out of real businesses all his life, with his share of successes and failures. I respect him and have learned much from him over the years as a solid businessman.

But do you know what I truly find compelling about Jim? It's that he's been really good at keeping at least one side gig at all times.

Have you ever seen that quatrefoil shape on the front of a typical suburban McMansion? Or the stucco-covered moldings around the windows on the outside of nice homes? Or how about the interior and exterior columns you see in newer tract homes? Well, as you probably already know, these things are not made of solid concrete. They're typically made of polystyrene foam or plaster. Jim spent a season of his business career in construction, mounting those decorative facades on the inside and outside of homes. Mounting foam shapes to houses is tricky. This is where Jim's story gets interesting. Jim needed glue to hold these things together. Very special glue.

Since these items are made of foam or lightweight material, the foam has to be cut and assembled into shapes, columns, window boxes, and the like. The polystyrene components are then glued to each other to hold their shape. Then the shape is glued to the wall, for example. Or, glued to a pole to create a column.

The glue that adheres the foam pieces to other foam pieces isn't the same as the common mastics used for other aspects of construction. The foam-to-foam gluing must be done with a unique product. Well, Jim found that product a long time ago. It wasn't really made for this particular purpose. Nevertheless, he found a source for this glue, and began buying it in 50-gallon drums for about $100 each.

Jim used it for his own business for many years. He ran into other people in the construction industry who needed this type of glue as well. Instead of just telling them where they could get their own 50-gallon drum, Jim told them he could get it *for* them in five-gallon buckets for $50 each. These other guys were ecstatic. They needed smaller volumes, and $50 for five gallons seemed cheap, considering that a one-gallon can of generic construction mastic runs $25, and that this specialty glue is unique and hard to find.

Even after Jim sold the construction business and moved onto other ventures, he kept buying that special glue and putting it into five-gallon buckets with his own label and selling it to contractors who needed it.

Here's how that worked: Jim would take a monthly trip to procure a 50-gallon drum of glue from the supplier. He would bring it home in his pickup truck and then pump it into smaller five-gallon buckets. He'd stick his own label on the buckets and sell them for $50 each. One hundred dollars for the glue for $100 would yield $500 in gross income, and a tidy profit of $400.

Some months Jim would sell just one drum ($400); other months he would sell four ($1,600). His total time commitment each month was two hours of driving in his truck, and then an hour or two to fill the buckets.

Jim sold his construction business many years ago, but he keeps this reliable little "candy store" running like a dream. He might use up to one hour per week to keep orders filled, but his overall commitment is never more than four to six hours per month. He can run this little side gig in the evenings or on weekends. He never loses a wink of sleep over the glue and his capital investment is only $100 to buy an entire drum, which he makes back immediately. Jim substantially improved his life for the past decade by making his secret glue into a side gig that earns anywhere from $400 to $1,600 per month.

Consider how hard it is to earn this sort of cash at a "regular" job! Let's do the math: If you take a full-time job at a convenience store at $10 per hour, your gross pay is $1,600 per month, and you only take-home about $1,200. And don't forget, you'd have to work a full-time schedule to bring that in! Jim could easily make that much every month for just *one hour per week.* He makes in four hours what a minimum wage worker earns in 160 hours!

Side gigs come with other benefits, too. Since Jim uses a corporate entity to run his side gig, that means it was technically a "business," but because it follows my rules of a *non*-business he isn't truly running a real business at all. However, the corporation provides Jim with a way to write off part of his auto expenses, an occasional meal with contractor customers, maybe even a round of golf with his customers. He could pay his cell phone bill through the business entity, and ultimately pay far less taxes, making his side gig even more profitable.

You might be seeing dollar signs here and ask, "Can't Jim make this bigger and make a killing? What's to prevent him from doing ten times the volume?" This is a question we'll see often as we evaluate side gigs. Some side gigs *can* become a million dollar business, others can't. And that's okay!

What if Jim tried to turn this side gig into a real business? This is where it's important to see the difference between a business and a side gig. ***Side gigs often don't scale well … and that's just fine for most side gigs***.

Scale, you ask. What does that mean?

Scalability is the ability of a business to increase its size while not decreasing profitability. According to Wikipedia, "Scalability is the ability of a system, network, or process to handle a growing amount of work in a capable manner or its ability to be enlarged to accommodate that growth." Let me use Jim's glue gig as an example. Can Jim take his nifty little side hustle and increase its size, let's say by ten or twenty times? In a good month, he already makes a tidy profit on four barrels. But will the monthly profit remain just as good on *eighty* barrels? The answer is no. The business is not scalable. Let's examine why.

If Jim has eighty barrels to handle, he'll need staff, or at least one full-time person. He'll then need to be sure he has worker's compensation insurance, a payroll service, and a liability insurance policy. He'll have to spend more time managing that employee. He'll need an office or warehouse. Jim will have to engage an accounting firm to do his books, and pay more to handle his taxes. Since his truck will be used daily to procure the drums of glue, he'll have to deal with higher fuel and insurance costs. He'll have an increase in his loss to bad debt as well. With a small customer base, Jim has never had a deadbeat client or he'd never sell them glue again.

But at eighty barrels he'd be selling four hundred buckets of glue per month, increasing his chances of bad debt.

His income would also fluctuate. Selling four barrels of glue a month only creates small swings in demand. But selling twenty times the volume will increase the volatility, and may create cash flow issues he didn't have when he was only dealing in four barrels per month. Jim may also face new pressures from competition, which would all be vying for the same customers; this could force down his prices. In the end, Jim's business would probably do all right. But even assuming he could get that much business, the profit would not come with the same margin. And more importantly, Jim would now be running the business full time.

Side gigs often do not scale well. But remember, if you are okay with the side gig just staying a side gig, then it is perfectly fine that it doesn't scale. Don't worry that it won't scale! You don't have to think about it if you never plan to grow it into the next billion dollar brand. If you want your side gig to become something bigger, then you should step back and reassess the scalability of your business. If not, then let your side gig find its equilibrium at a small size, in which operations conform to a non-business matrix. Small and non-scalable can be perfect.

To summarize, keep these advantageous factors in mind as we progress:

- Small initial capital outlay
- Little or no ongoing capital needed
- Little time required
- Steady income
- Low risk/liability
- Low stress

Jim's glue gig clearly qualifies. But if you extrapolate it to a full-scale business, you can see that it would not meet any of the above criteria. A full-time glue business would require capital, time, increase risk and stress, and ultimately lower profits and create more ups and downs.

It's just fine to have a side gig that can scale into a million dollar company. However, if you want to live the life I have in Bali, or you want to keep your day job, then you don't need a business that scales. You want one that fits our "side gig matrix." Small side gigs can be awesome, and provide steady income for years or decades without turning into full-time companies.

Exercises:

Write down your answers to the following questions using the prompts you see below. Then put them aside for later in the book:

- What have you done in the past? (List freely without editing!)
- Consider your contacts: What they might buy from you?
- Consider your sources for products: Is there something you can access for a much cheaper price than others are able to?
- Is there something you know really well that others don't know as well?
    - Think of your past employment and/or businesses.
    - Think of what you have become an expert in.
- Think about what causes stress: Write down the things you don't like to do that causes stress. (For some, this might be talking to people you don't know; for others it could be working alone in silence with no one to talk to. Ponder these categories and write down the things that are stress triggers. This will be important later in the book when we go looking for a side gig that's perfect for you.

Chapter 5

“Do What You Love" and Other Bad Advice

Are you pumped up to "*do what you love*"?!!!

Are you ready to pour your passion into something that will *change the world?!!!*

Good. Go to see a motivational speaker, and let us know how that works out for ya :-)

Look, I’m about to tell you goes against everything you may have heard from daytime TV talk shows and various self-help books, but this is some serious Truth we're bringing you.

So here it is.

You want to do something you love? Make some money first.

Here's why: If you want to get control of your time, you’ve got to get control of your money.

And to get control of your money, you’ve got to do something that makes money.

You know all those gurus selling you the myth that you should "do what you love and the money will follow?"

It’s bad advice.

It’s the advice from people who have already hit a home run and now have the luxury to sit back and reflect on more lofty matters, while forgetting what really matters to the rest of us.

And that’s money, honey.

That's right, we are here with some tough love today.

You can't very well be the social entrepreneur who saves the world until you've saved yourself.

You don't need to feed the poor as part of your business plan.

You don't need to advance the kingdom for Jesus' sake as part of your side gig.

You don't need to make your money a result of good deeds, a political agenda or a New Age journey toward enlightenment.

If that's you, then take it from me: You can still be the good believer, the seeker, the helper, and the guru, that's all fine.

But you need to do it while you *do something that makes money.* You simply can't let your more exalted ambitions drive what you do. Instead, *let them motivate your why.*

So why DO you want to make money?

Is it so that you can help the world, advance a cause, or save mankind from itself?

Great. Make your money the way money gets made ... and let your passions permeate wherever else they may be.

Here's a story that will bring this home to you ...

I had a friend who was a passionate scuba diver. He would do scuba tours around the world and made a bit of money on them as well. In the early 2000s he decided to launch a scuba website because he wanted to launch a business that revolved around doing what he loved.

But guess what?

He didn't love web development. He didn't love marketing.

He didn't love scheduling, customer service, financial management, and every other aspect of business.

In fact, he wasn't doing much of *anything* he loved. It turns out all the requirements of owning a business robbed him of all his time in the water.

This is true for so many people who insist on getting into ventures centering on their so-called passions.

Whether it's golf, wine, restaurants, food, fashion, or gardening, the reality is that business and side gigs should be about making money ... NOT about doing what you think you love.

For some of you, this will feel like a presidential pardon. You're free, my friend. Go forth and make some moolah.

For others, it could be a shock to your system. The ultimate buzz-kill. Maybe you've been spinning your wheels for years on this fantasy.

If this describes you, then it's going to be hard to let it go. You might not like me right now (sad face).

But listen, I'm here to help you for one reason, and one reason only: ***To live life on your own terms.***

And when you do achieve that, then you'll have some control over your time and your money and you can go see Tony

Robbins and get inspired to spend some of your time and money doing cool shit that saves the world.

But for now? Don't ever forget that the world is full of plumbers and electricians who do their part to make the world a better place. Why are you so special?

Can you not market and create a website around how, say, to keep orchids alive? Would you feel like you are missing your calling?

Look, if you really want to "Be the Change," then start with the little stuff. Start with making a difference in your family by making enough money to take control back from The Man.

Forget for now what you *love*. Instead, ***do what you are good at.*** Leverage it any way you can. And expand your network.

That's the formula for success.

Use what you've got inside. And use what you've got outside.

That may have sounded vague, so let me explain what I mean by that.

Inside, you've got some skills. Talent. Work experience. Aptitude.

Outside, you've got some assets. Your network, for example. It might be a little network right now, but that's okay, you start there. Your network is an asset that you can leverage to identify a side gig that you can do that makes money fast.

Bottom line: It's all about your skills *and* your network. That's the foundation upon which you base your side gig or business. Not doing what you love.

ACTION STEP:

Add your skills and add your network to your brainstorming pad. If you are using my Side Gig Calculator, take a look at these three worksheets:

Worksheet No. 1: Do What You Like

This sheet lets you play with the idea of doing what you like (see, I'm not a not complete killjoy!) This sheet is an objective way of ensuring you don't wind up unhappy like my scuba diver buddy.

Worksheet No. 2: Do What You Are Good At

This sheet lets you analyze and play with your skills to be sure you focus on a side gig that deploys your best and most valuable abilities.

Worksheet No. 3: Do What Others Can Help You With.

This sheet measures your network. You'll list five people who might be helpful to your particular side gig efforts, and then you'll see how each one objectively rates so that you can reach out most effectively.

Chapter 6

Web Businesses

I told you about how I built a website called freelegalaid.com. Businesses based on the Internet tend to be good side gigs. You can do it from anywhere, and you can have more than one web-based side gig that you operate simultaneously. Let me tell you how I ended up with a second side gig a few years ago. This one fell in my lap, but sometimes that's how you end up with a side gig. It can just be a wonderful coincidence.

LetterPOP

Three of my good friends had launched a startup around 2006. They raised money from investors, and put almost two years of their time into developing an online newsletter creator called LetterPOP.

LetterPOP was launched at a time when the big competitors were placing their bets on customer management tools and services (known as CRM), rather than on newsletter creation software like LetterPOP.

My friends' gamble did not pay off. Two years and several hundred thousand dollars later, LetterPOP was not generating a sustainable profit.

The team decided to shut it down. In the last chapter, I described how side gigs don't usually scale *up* into full businesses. Likewise, full-blown businesses don't often scale *down* to side gig status.

In other words, there was no easy way my friends could operate LetterPOP as a side gig. It was a business that required programmers, management, customer service, and an aggressive plan for growth. So they chose to close the business and sell the site. As you will see later in these pages, many "failed" startups end up in this condition. Many startups reach a point in which they cannot sustain the business under their original model and they end up selling their assets. Many such websites end up on auction sites like Flippa, where existing domains and websites are auctioned and sold at bargain basement prices.

LetterPOP would have ended up on the auction block on a site like Flippa — but for one person: me. Before they put it up for grabs for bidders, the team offered to sell the website to me. I said yes and purchased it for $6,000 — a fair price for a website that never found adequate profitability — and moved it to my own server.

What did I do with this failed startup? Simple. I cut the fat and made it a side gig.

I immediately started making as much as $1,000 per month. And I'm here to tell you that *you* can find just as good of a deal if you go hunting, as we will discuss later in this book.

How did I pull this off? Well, my costs were essentially zero. The income is derived entirely from paid subscriptions. (Even now, if you want to go use the site, you can pay as little as $4.95 per year for the basic subscription.)

What does it require of me? Not much! I host the website. I answer trouble tickets from customers (one or two per week). And I occasionally post helpful content to the blog.

I keep it lean on purpose. Sure, I could invest considerable time into running it. I could also invest a lot of money into updating the software. But I don't want to make this into a full business again. The business failed as a full-scale business. The better move was to make it a passive business, and not support it at all, and just let the site make a regular monthly income that requires only about an hour of my time each month.

In exchange for about one hour of my time per month, I can just sit back and let LetterPOP bring in steady money, month after month, year after year, in additional income.

That's what I call a classic side gig. Together with Freelegalaid.com, I'm able to collect a substantial monthly income without working more than an hour per week. Not a bad duo of side gigs, right? You too can have more than one side gig, particularly if your side gigs are web-based businesses that require very little of your time to maintain the site.

But I'm not the only one with multiple Internet side gigs. Let's look at my buddy John.

John's Web Tools

A good friend of mine is a web programmer. His *real* business is selling his time to companies that want to deploy large-scale web projects. He is very good at what he does, and he commands a high hourly rate. However, he doesn't have to work much, and regularly turns down work that comes his way. He can do this because he has side gigs that empower him to make choices about what to do with his time.

A couple of years ago, I saw a Facebook post John shared. He was taking thirty days off from all other activities to teach himself to draw. I happened to see him the next day, so I brought it up.

"John, I saw your post on Facebook. Are you teaching yourself to draw?"

"Yeah," he said. "I'm doing one drawing a day for thirty days. It will force me to gain some drawing skills in a short period of time."

"How much time will this take each day?" I asked.

"Oh. All day."

"What a minute," I said. "You're going to do nothing for thirty days but *draw*?"

"Yup. That's the idea."

"Don't you need to work? You know, make money to pay the bills?"

"Nope. My website is doing well. I'll be fine," he said.

My jaw dropped. I knew that John had a bit of side income from a website he owned. But I didn't think he could take off an entire month and learn to draw. By the way, he is now an incredible artist. He finds that art is meditative and enjoys the skills he would not have acquired if he hadn't taken those 30 days to master the baseline tools for art.

What is John's side gig? John runs a website that gives away free tools to edit photos. And it turns out that John's website gets millions of monthly visitors. That high traffic translates into a steady stream of advertising income from Google Adsense, along with other income from posters, printed material and even donations that come through the website. I don't know how exactly much John makes, but I can tell you that he can take a month off and do nothing but learn to draw! His website is the perfect side gig.

John's site doesn't require very much work; it's not a full time job. While he did have to spend some of his spare time early on to build it, the site did not require any capital outlay and it does not require any ongoing capital investment. He never loses sleep over it. In fact, this side gig has now been steadily generating an income for a decade, and it continues to this day.

What has John done with this money? Well, as you've already seen, he improved himself by becoming an artist. He also took time to build other software apps that required large blocks of time to set up. However, once he launches an app, it makes more money without much additional work. One of those apps, for instance, took his full-time attention for several months. But here's the thing: *He could afford the time because his side gig was paying him enough to cover his expenses while he built more web and software products.*

At one point John had a paid mobile app that sold over a thousand downloads per month (at $2.99 per download). In case you're keeping count, that's three side gigs making thousands of dollars per month each. John essentially doesn't have to work if he doesn't want to.

John sometimes does software development work as a "real" business. Because of the success of his non-businesses, he has the freedom to accept jobs he enjoys and can choose to work only with people he likes. Or, he can just take thirty days off to learn how to draw and not work at all. He gets to act like a guy who doesn't need the money because, well, he *doesn't* need the money. His side gigs allow him to keep away from stressful, unpleasant projects. The value of that lifestyle can hardly be underestimated.

You might think that John's story is unique because he is a professional programmer. But don't forget *my* story. I'm certainly not a professional programmer, and my side gigs are websites, too. You don't need to be a programmer to have an Internet-based side gig. Let me give you some other examples of web-based non-businesses that are owned by people who don't program computer software for a living.

Steve's Stubs

Have you ever known one of those people who *never* seems to work? You go to the gym in the middle of the day, and there he is again. He's working out, he's chatting with someone and moving at a pace that tells you he doesn't have to be anywhere in particular. Or you see him often when you stop for groceries, except he's not wearily cruising the aisles with a loosened necktie with that battered, end-of-day look. He's still in his gym clothes with time to burn. You see him down at the park or beach and you can tell he's truly *there*. It's like he doesn't have to worry about money. I know a few of these guys. One of their secrets is that they have a side gig, but they *don't* have a main gig. That's their little secret: Find the perfect side gig, and instead of making more money and spending more money, enjoy the simple life and do what you want most of the day ... *every day*.

Steve is in this special little "off-the-clock" fraternity. I had known him for years before I discovered his secret. I saw him at the gym, seemingly with the freedom to be there every day, whenever he pleased, chatting people up, taking his sweet time. I, on the other hand, would have precisely 40 minutes to cram in a workout before I had run off to a meeting. Walking out, I'd see him casually eating lunch near the gym. In the evening, he would jog down my street. I live near the beach and often take a walk on the sand. Guess who would be down there watching the sunset or playing volleyball? Yup, Steve.

How does a guy in his mid-twenties spend all of his time at leisure? He must have a family trust fund or something, right? Nope. He has a side gig, and just a side gig. No job. No "real" business.

Now, guys like Steve don't just come out and reveal their secrets. It took a while before I got him to share his secret side gig. It's pretty simple, actually. He buys and sells tickets. He stumbled into the business with a friend. As they learned and collaborated, they discovered there was a market for buying and selling tickets to concerts, sporting events and other events. How is it possible that Steve and his buddy can both make a living with competing, massive markets like StubHub? Well, an important lesson in business is that where someone is already successfully doing something, there is typically room for others. Just because there already are large websites facilitating ticket resale does not mean that you cannot play in the same sandbox, too. Sometimes people just want to list their tickets on Craigslist and wait for someone like Steve to come pick them up and pay cash in-person.

Now I would not recommend that you rush out and copy Steve. Steve found a niche at a time and place that worked for his aptitude. It may not work for you. In fact, by now Steve has a significant advantage over newcomers. He has been peddling stubs long enough to learn the market. His trained eye can instantly spot steals on tickets from Comic-Con to Coachella. He has the honed wisdom of a stock trader, allowing him to carefully buy and sell in a way that keeps his side gig humming along profitably.

Now that you know the specifics of Steve's secret side gig, don't miss the bigger picture: What makes Steve special is that he lives a life ***with only a side gig***. For others, living the good life means having more time, and not necessarily more money.

You might be thinking, "Hey Steve, why not keep the side gig and go make *another* $50,000 per year with a day job? Why be content with one modest income when you could have two?" Not a bad question, and there may come a day when Steve *does* decide to make more money. But for now, Steve is the master of his time, making enough to do what he wants, when he wants. Sure, Steve could take a day job and earn more money. But to what end? A nicer car? Purchase a condo instead of renting an apartment? Travel or eat out more often? Steve doesn't want those things. Steve wants to play beach volleyball and go hit a concert with his girlfriend. Steve rides a skateboard to the gym — why would he want an expensive car? Steve's side gig *already* gives him the life of a millionaire. He doesn't need more money to buy the thing he already has, which is time freedom. That's plenty enough for an amazing lifestyle.

Julie's Coupon Sites

I met Julie at a networking event several years ago. She was in her late twenties, married with one toddler. She and her husband both had jobs. They worked too much, and made too little. Julie searched for the right side gig for about a year, spending most of that time watching auctions on a website called Flippa. As I mentioned earlier in the book, Flippa is a large platform for buying and selling domain names and websites.

Julie wanted to buy an existing website. Her goal was to find a website that had a history of making steady money, but was something that could be grown over time. She started by just browsing the listings on Flippa every few days. If she found an interesting site for sale, she would ask questions, and then watch for the final selling price. This helped her understand what she could expect to pay when she eventually purchased a site of her own.

She spent about a year watching the market and learning. Her year of reconnaissance served her well. She learned about various types of websites, how much they made, as well as how much time each would take to run. She learned that many of the websites were projects that someone else had spent years working on. Most of the sites cost the original owner far more than they were selling for. For example, one of the sites she followed was founded by two developers who spent one year and $50,000 creating it. The site could be purchased for $20,000 or less. That same site was making $3,000 per month with little effort. Julie was learning that if she found the right deal, she could make most of her investment back within a few months, and then everything else would be profit. Of course, if she could get a deal like that, and also grow it by running the business better, then she could make her money back sooner and enjoy an even greater profit.

Once she understood what she wanted and what different websites were worth, she went to work bidding on websites.

When I met Julie, she had acquired not one, but two websites that were making steady income with very little of her time. I can't share with you exactly what she paid, but, I can say that she made her money back within a few months, just like she'd planned.

She started by buying one site in the "coupon" market. The site had high traffic and steady revenue. She quickly started watching Flippa for other coupon websites and found another that she managed to acquire soon after. Because she was able to combine these two related sites effectively, she created something that was greater than the sum of its parts. For her 1 + 1 = 3. The websites recouped her investment in less than six months, and after a year in the business she had quit her day job and was making more than her old salary working only a few hours per week. In fact, she told me her husband had come to her with a job application. He asked if he could quit his job and work for her. No joke. She was considering it. He wanted to get in on what Julie had created. She had it easy with her new side gig. She could spend time with her toddler, and enjoy the freedom of making what she did full-time while not working much at all.

How Can These Examples Apply to *Your* Side Gig?

Let's look at some of the lessons learned from the examples so far. Each web business has a different revenue model to consider.

Freelegalaid.com makes money from advertising. The key to Freelegalaid.com's success is that

It's content directly correlates to targeted ads. Freelegalaid.com runs ads provided by Google's Adsense network, and because the users on Freelegalaid.com are interested in legal assistance, they are shown ads related to what they are reading. When you have a site that partners with advertising networks (such as Google Adsense) to automatically display ads that generate shared revenue, having very specific, industry-related content for those advertisers makes all the difference. Tightly focused relevance is king. Informational websites should cater content to advertisers in high-paying industries. Those include: mortgages or loans, travel, car donations, attorneys, credit repair, credit cards and balance transfers, classes and degrees, medical treatment, software and hosting, and data recovery. You'll earn more by building around those subjects than if you center your sites on more "niche-y", less valuable topics. There is still plenty of room for you to create a website with useful content and generate money with advertising income. Blogs, video training, how-to sites, curated news content, and many other types of websites are making money every day for people just like you.

In addition to making money from ads, you can use a website to make money selling products. Yes, some people sell actual products as part of their side gig. For example, you could sell jewelry on Etsy.com. My friend John has a site with millions of users that lets customers make inspirational posters. So he receives ad revenue, much like Freelegalaid.com does. But the customer can also order the physical, printed poster. When someone does that, he makes money. He doesn't have to print or mail the posters either. He uses a third-party service that receives the orders and drop-ships the products directly to the customers. John just provides the platform for a user to edit photos and turn them into something, such as inspirational posters, calendars or postcards. Once you order the poster, it is all handled by a printer that pays John, and ships the poster directly to the customer. This is just one example of many in which you can sell an item you don't ever have to store, pack or ship. All you do is create an affiliate relationship with someone else who sells products, and you get paid a hefty commission for making the sale. Commission Junction (cj.com) is one of the largest networks of affiliate products and services in the world. Join CJ and explore the types of products and services you can sell, and that may even help you figure out the kind of website you can develop for your side gig.

LetterPOP is an example of a third type of revenue you can make from a website. It makes income from paid user subscriptions. It offers good software, has a solid customer base, and produces a modest-but-steady income. It's ridiculously low entry price of $4.99 annually per customer doesn't hurt either. Subscription-based websites are nice because they don't rely on advertising income. However, the product must be higher quality because users are paying for it. If a website is free to users, they will tolerate a lower quality product and customers will also put up with ads. If the site charges a fee, then the content or software must be higher caliber. Consider building a site that has free options with ads, and then a premium option without ads that charges a monthly subscription. We call this a "freemium" option, and it allows you to generate income from ads for the free users, and then monthly recurring revenue from the paid users.

Julie's coupon sites are making money from more than one revenue source. She gets advertising income much like Freelegalaid.com, but she also can send targeted offers to users through email, and sell other people's products and services as an affiliate and get paid a commission.

Julie's example also teaches us that research is important. Don't rush out tomorrow and buy a website. Take your time. Watch and learn. Network and find out what others are doing. In fact, Julie was at my networking event for that very purpose. She wanted to learn more and discover ways she could expand her side gig. She wanted to meet marketing and SEO experts, and perhaps collaborate or partner with others who had complementary businesses. Do your due diligence and don't stop learning.

Julie's story also tells us that a side gig can be purchased rather than started from scratch. Freelegalaid.com, Steve's Stubs, and John's portal all started from nothing. This can take years and is fraught with risk. (Fortunately, in those examples almost no cash was required to launch them, meaning the risk was mostly about time, not money.) But look at that advantage of Julie's method: It paid off much more quickly. She took a business already built with someone else's sweat and cash. She could waltz in and snap up the whole shebang for a relative song. Same thing with LetterPOP, which was an existing site with revenue coming in; it paid for itself in six months.

Also keep in mind that Julie's side gig did not require much up-front capital. Yes, she spent more than $20,000, but she and her husband had jobs, as well as savings and investments. So for her that amount was not a major up-front investment. For many people, of course, this is far too much. Don't lose heart! The good news is that you can find worthy sites on Flippa for far less. You might not be able to make $3,000 per month right away, but you can still find similar scenarios to Julie's if you start hunting and follow the same principles. Find a website that makes $300 per month and buy it for $2,000. That way the site has paid for itself in seven months, or even less, if you're able to grow the income through your own effort.

ACTION STEPS

Start watching auction sites like Flippa

- Search Flippa for existing sites, not just domain names.
- Search for sites making more than $300 per month.
- Read the comments, feel free to ask questions.
- Watch the auction to see the ultimate sale price.

- Track the auctions separately and log the asking price, the income and the final sales price.

If necessary, get over any fear of technology

- Watch video courses on hosting and setting up WordPress.
- Use third-party site builders like SquareSpace and Wix.
- Consider paying someone to help you do your first site.
- Pay someone for helping maintain your site, but not until you actually understand what is going on by doing it yourself.

Brainstorm: What is your expertise?

- What content could you write dozens of pages about?
- What is your passion?
- What are you really good at (even if it's not your passion)?
- Categorize the above into separate headings and brainstorm about what makes each subject unique.
- Search for websites that blog, podcast or publish content around these subjects and put the websites under each heading.

- Note the difference, if any, between your content and the content you find on the web.
- Star any content that fits into these categories: mortgages or loans, travel, car donations, attorneys, credit repair, credit cards and balance transfers, classes and degrees, medical treatment, software and hosting, and data recovery.
- If you have content that is not in these areas that you could create, then research the value of ads for your type of content. What's hot changes with time.

Chapter 7

The Hobby Side Gig

If you have a hobby and want to turn it into a business, you can! Many people take their hobby and turn it into a profitable side gig.

Sometimes it becomes a perfect fit. Remember, a side gig should be low on capital requirements, generate steady cash flow, require only a little of your time, and not add to your stress. Many hobbies fit that profile perfectly. Hobbies don't require much cash, and can create steady cash flow without much time or stress. (Let's face it, if your hobby causes you undue stress, it's time to find a new one!)
What sort of hobbies make good side gigs? Let me show you a few examples.

Erica's Animals

Erica has a bit of an animal addiction. An animal lover since early youth, she not only figured out how to keep her pets alive but how to breed them as well. Unlike me (who could never keep goldfish alive, let alone hamsters, and even my bunnies didn't reproduce), Erica has the magic touch. She's bred everything from spiders (yikes, right?) to bunnies to exotic cats. She not only has an obvious love for animals, but a passion for the breeding process as well. If a side gig centering on breeding seemed inevitable, well, one could be excused for thinking it was baked into her DNA.

By the time I got to know Erica, she had moved her way up the breeding chain. She had done really well with dogs for many years, and she made a fairly decent amount of money. But her passion moved from canines to horses. And when you get into horses, you are now into a very expensive hobby.

Erica's penchant for expensive horses could have become her financial ruin. But her preoccupation with pets became an occupation. A profitable one at that. Rather than just owning expensive pets for the fun of it, Erica owns them, loves them, feeds them, and breeds them. Take her $2,000 dog: Five litters later, that's $50,000 worth of adorable cuteness.

Horses are a bigger gamble, but once a horse has certain certifications, a male can be put to stud for quite a lot of money. Once the horse has proven to be a good income stream, you can sell a horse for a lot more, say, $50,000 for a horse that may have cost you $10,000. So a horse can be a source of income in two ways: from selling its stud services, which creates an ongoing source of income, and as a substantial payday when the horse is sold.

Erica's hobby not only supports the ongoing ownership and breeding of horses, but it also generates income that makes a nice little side gig for her family. She enjoys the combined benefit of being able to buy and enjoy her animals (a hobby), and making a nice side living to boot. This side gig isn't a full-time job. If it was, she'd likely work far more and make less per hour for her time. She'd have to buy insurance, deal with liabilities, hire staff, buy software, deal with licensing and permits, and a host of other things that don't worry her at this stage. She's an animal owner who knows how to pick the right animals, breed them and make a little side gig income while enjoying her hobby.

Woodworking for Pay and Pleasure

I was raised by wonderful parents who have a very high aptitude for mechanical dexterity. My dad worked on cars from the time he was a boy. Legend has it that he was fixing up a car when he was only ten years old. He also learned metalwork before high school, and woodwork became a hobby he picked up along the way. My mom was raised by a handy father, making her just as handy as my father. Whether by nurture or by nature, I ended up with a rather broad set of mechanical skills. I've rebuilt car engines and lawn mower engines. As a kid, I built forts and go-karts from scratch. I rehabbed an electric car when I was 15. And it should come as no surprise that I learned woodworking from my dad.

I'm not one to make woodworking a personal hobby, although I have used those skills to build furniture and refinish items. My father, however, was an avid woodworker. It was a hobby that let him create furniture he couldn't have afforded to buy otherwise. It saved our family plenty on furniture, cabinets and shelves. But my dad also extended these skills outside the home, doing woodworking for others.

I have a feeling my Dad eventually stopped doing woodworking because it was less fun once he *had* to do it for these side projects. But for a season of his life, he had a side gig in woodworking. My mom had a similar period with stained glass. She sold custom leaded glass, and also sold pre-made pieces at street fairs.

Woodworking and leaded glass would have been terrible businesses as a real, "full-fledged" endeavors. Why? Because they would have needed to scale to a certain level of production, and then find broader channels of distribution, such as trade shows or flea markets. Then they would have had to spend much of the income to promote their products, maybe even hire people. The hobbyist joy would have been sanded down like so much sawdust. And the business probably would not have flourished. They would have had to compete with others who could make cabinets or stained glass cheaper and faster. Over time they surely would have been forced to lower their prices, eroding their profitability.

However, as a *side gig?* That was a way to park their hobbies at the corner of Joy and Fulfillment, with the helpful gravy of a few hundred extra dollars coming in every month from paid projects.

Bob the Builder

Let me give you another hobby example. My friend Bob enjoys doing tile work. (Honest, he really does!) For him, tile work is a labor of love. And every now and then someone he knows asks him to do some tile work. His fee is more than fair, and his friends know he is good at it. He does it because he thinks it is fun. When he's on his hands and knees with a trowel on someone's bathroom floor, he's merely doing something he would already do for free. But he gets paid for it. That, my friends, is a win-win.

What if Bob got a contractor's license and started Bob's Tile Company? That would turn his hobby into a business. He would then have to carry license and insurance. Competitive bidding would squeeze his prices down. He would have to use all of his time to run the business. But as a side gig, he works when and how he wants, and gets paid whatever price he asks.

Cindy's Catering

Cindy has a full-time job operating a business she owns. But she also loves to cook. Cooking is a hobby for her, a real passion. And she has turned her hobby into profit by doing small catering jobs as well as gigs as small as cooking for two. She charges a reasonable fee to be the "private chef" for those who want to host a special dinner for a friend or a date. Cindy gets to cook her heart out on someone else's dime, and then makes a couple hundred dollars for just a few hours work. When she caters a larger event, the profit is even higher.

The best part for Cindy is that she has total control over whether she takes a catering or private chef job. If her business is busy, or she has other obligations, she can just decline to take work. If she has the time, then she can make the extra cash while doing something she absolutely loves. For her, it's also meditative; she gets to put her mind to something other than her day job. And of course she gets to eat some delicious food along the way!

Tanner's Dog Sitting

Tanner is a dog lover. He's also a bachelor. He tripped across a wonderful side gig a few years ago: dog sitting. His duties aren't restricted to just hanging out with a dog. He'll actually live in the homes of busy people who travel a lot. When I met him, he was house-sitting a million-dollar house overlooking the ocean. The homeowner was a busy businessman who often traveled to Europe. He had two dogs in the house that needed more than just dog-sitting. They needed a person who was there to be the foster-parent to the dogs for weeks at a time.

What did Tanner get for this? He got to live rent-free, and got paid a weekly rate as well. He also was paid a small stipend for food. He walked the dogs twice a day and did freelance work from his computer to make even more money. If he sounds like a real side gig hustler, well, you'd be right. Tanner loved the dogs, and they loved him. Even when the owner was in town, Tanner could stay in the house if he wanted. He would not get his dog-sitting pay when the owner was home. But he enjoyed free rent! Tanner also had three other families in the neighborhood who paid him a daily fee to check on their dogs once per day and take them for a walk. I once saw him with a troupe of five dogs walking through the neighborhood! He smiled and we both laughed. He was laughing his way all the way to the bank.

Need more examples of side gigs? I know a guy who does metalwork and performs small welding jobs for extra money. And I know of more than one artist who takes paid work or has some other means to monetize their art. Think of the quilting enthusiast who sells her quilts. Or the jewelry maker hobbyist who has an Etsy store for her wares. These side gigs, and many more like them, are grounded in the pride and joy of an enjoyable — and *profitable* — craft. And none of them are endeavors that should be upgraded to business class. Make it a side gig, enjoy it, and make some extra cash along the way.

Consider your hobbies. Do you do something unique that might have value to someone else? Can you do just enough of it to create a few hundred dollars per month while following the rules for a side gig?

Remember, side gigs don't require a lot of capital outlay. Translation: Don't use the side gig as an excuse to go out and buy thousands of dollars in equipment! If you already have it, then fine. If you need to put a lot of cash into a side gig, then you have to step back and consider if you are trying to start a real business rather than a *non*-business side gig.

If you can't make your hobby into a side gig, that's fine, too. Not all hobbies make great side gigs. But if you can, then it could be the easiest pathway to a profitable side gig.

Wedding Planner Story

Bob the builder loved to lay tile so much he would do it for free, right? Well, Jo was the same way with planning events. She loved it, and did it as a favor whenever she could. She found a steady stream of people through her church who needed help. She volunteered to coordinate any wedding where there was not already a planner involved. This gave Jo a wealth of experience, and it also brought her joy by doing something she really loved.

Eventually, Jo was able to begin charging a small fee to those who could afford her service. Through her years of planning-as-hobby, she met many people in the wedding industry and built a reputation with other service providers. That network eventually provided referrals and highly paid wedding gigs outside her church community. Her hobby turned into a well-paid side gig. And she makes more than most fully employed people, while working far less.

Carlos' Photography

Carlos has spent years learning photography. He honed his craft on the beaches of San Diego. He owned the best equipment, and would practice his photography by taking photos of the natural settings around San Diego. He would also help friends with free photography when he could. These included occasional portraits, amateur models needing portfolios, product shots for websites, and more. It was a hobby, but it was a serious hobby. He knew he wanted to eventually turn this hobby into a business.

For most of his career, he was a veterinary assistant. However, working full-time did not allow him to pursue his dreams. So, one day he started doing canine teeth cleaning on the side. People loved him, dogs loved him. And he was able to stop working and just survive on his side gig, performing canine oral hygiene. But it got even better. You see, once he replaced his full-time job with a side gig, he was able to throw himself into his photography. His work blossomed. He gathered his best pieces, and started selling the photographs as large-scale art. He focused on his beach scenes, which are popular with both locals and tourists. Companies now buy his large photos mounted on metal for installation in office lobbies and restaurants. He also has two galleries, and his art is becoming well known. And as you might guess, he still does a little canine hygiene on the side. Why give up an easy side gig?

ACTION STEPS

Brainstorm your past and present hobbies. Here's a list of hobbies to get you thinking:

- Jewelry
- Sewing
- Woodwork
- Metalwork

- Art And Graphic Art
- Auto Work
- Copy Editing/Proofreading
- Cooking
- Dog Sitting
- Dog Grooming
- Specialty Gardening
- Music Instructor (Guitar, Piano, Etc)
- Sports Coach (Tennis, Golf, Etc)
- Educational Tutoring
- Computer Repair
- Child Care

Assess your assets.

- Write down all of your hobbies.
- Write down the tools, equipment and supplies you have for your hobby.
-

Assess the value proposition and competition.

- Write down the prices you believe you can charge for your hobby products.
- Next, go find comparable products on the web, and write down those prices for comparison. Be sure you

find truly comparable products (i.e. handmade cutting boards that are made in the U.S.).

- Write down the alternative products and prices as well (i.e. handmade cutting boards from Indonesia).

Chapter 8

That Big Idea!

Aaron Krause was a typical American entrepreneur and inventor. His expertise was in the car wash and detail business. Over the years, he had come up with great ideas in that market and filed patents. One of his products was a buffing pad adapter with quick-connect technology. That product was eventually acquired by 3M. But 3M passed on a portfolio of patents related to a sponge that 3M simply didn't perceive to be valuable. Krause was left with that patent, and let it sit for nearly five years before taking it to *Shark Tank*, where he won an investment from Lori Grenier. That company, Sponge Daddy, is now available in Bed Bath & Beyond, Kroger, Home Depot, Ace Hardware, Walmart, Target, CVS, Wegmans, ShopRite and Giant, and sold 1.8 million units in a single day on QVC. Some say it is the most successful *Shark Tank*-funded project to date.

Shark Tank has brought patents to the forefront for aspiring entrepreneurs. I myself am an intellectual property attorney and help entrepreneurs identify and protect their IP. In today's business economy, the greatest asset most companies have is their intellectual property.

Most don't realize how much intellectual property alone can be the key to your success. Many patentable ideas can turn into a side gig that makes money, even if the idea doesn't turn into a billion-dollar consumer product.

If you find yourself hearing a lot about intellectual property these days, it's because IP is at the heart of most of today's businesses. Back in the 1970s and before, most of the value in a business existed in the tangible goods it owned. The value of a business might include inventory, trucks, land and machinery. A small portion of goodwill might be on the books, but most of the value was in its physical assets.

From the 1980s through today, however, there has been a massive shift in the U.S. away from physical assets toward intangible assets. Most of these intangible assets are what we refer to as intellectual property. Generally, IP is broken down into five types: Patents, trademarks, copyrights, trade secrets and rights of publicity. I'll briefly describe each one.

Patents cover useful inventions that are novel and nonobvious. A good example would be my brother-in-law Tim's patent for his "Silent Bag" business that you'll read about shortly; or Amazon's patent for its "1 Click" method; or (and I'm not kidding here), the patent for a 12-gauge golf driver. You can patent a lot of things. Tens of thousands of new patents are issued each year. They cost quite a bit to pursue because you have to pay attorneys. Once a patent is issued, it is good for 20 years if you pay the maintenance fees.

Trademarks cover brand-identifying things such as word trademarks, design trademarks, logos, and even the shape of a product or packaging (like the Coke bottle). Trademarks are an essential part of most businesses, and can even be an important to side gig businesses.

*Copyright la*w covers original works of authorship that are fixed in a tangible medium of expression. Think of books, poems, music, lyrics, sculptures, paintings, computer code, user interface design, digital images, video, audio and more. Copyright is implicated in almost everything you do every day. Every web page licenses you the right to view or use its content. Every video or movie you watch has copyrights attached to it. Everything you create also likely has copyright implications. If you create something, you probably own copyrights.

Trade secret law covers the protection of secrets, such as recipes, customer lists, business plans, or formulas and algorithms. Trade secrets protect the Colonel's secret recipe for fried chicken, the secret formula to Coke and the recipe for Monsanto's weed poison. If you have something that has value from being a secret, then you may have IP rights under trade secret law.

Finally, *rights of publicity* is a type of IP that protects a person's name, likeness and persona. Rights of publicity are mostly beneficial for celebrities. It also might protect you from having your face or voice used to sponsor or promote a product. If you do something that uses another person's image or name, then you are probably implicating rights of publicity law in some way.

Now that you've had a quick primer on IP law, let's talk about how IP law applies to the typical side gig or small business.

If you own a patent, then you have the right to exclude others from practicing the invention. This gives you a major competitive advantage because only you can do the thing you invented. In addition, your patent gives you the right to charge other people money if they want to use the patent. We call that a "license." You can practice your own patent or you can license it to a third-party.

You might invent and patent the next great invention, and build the product and sell it. You might simply get the patent and then find someone to license it from you. Either way, you can turn your great idea into a steady side gig, and possibly even hit a home run.

Your best chance of hitting upon a stroke of genius is an idea *within an industry that you already know well*, rather than some genius idea in a field you're not familiar with. Let me tell you about one patented product that shows how my brother-in-law created a side gig out of a single great idea.

Silent Bags ®

Tim is a prop guy in Hollywood. He's been in that business for a long time. Along the way he realized that the studio sets used highly sensitive microphones that pick up *any* little sound. Which means in the world of stage props, it's imperative to find props that don't make much noise or, alternatively, re-engineering existing props to make them quieter. One of the most noisy things on the typical movie set is a paper bag. Tim came up with the idea of using special materials to make bags that are silent but look exactly like a regular paper bag. He created the Silent Bag.

Tim happened to know someone in the intellectual property law business (ahem), and so with a little help he was able to get a patent on his product. In addition, he obtained a trademark for the brand Silent Bags. He has spent years making Silent Bags ® in his garage. He has been able to create a steady stream of revenue, every month for many years. In fact, as his kids grew up, they worked for him assembling bags in the garage, earning money and helping Tim so that he didn't have to spend *his* weekends building bags. The result? Tim has enjoyed a decade of side gig income while his kids developed a work ethic and learned entrepreneurship along the way.

Of course, as with many other side gigs, Tim also gets the benefit of tax deductions for his business operations. He can write off his home office, a portion of his mobile phone expenses, auto and meal expenses, and more. I don't know how much he makes, and it's none of my business, but let's use a random figure for hypothetical purposes of $800 per month. Then assume that Tim uses some of that income to pay for business meals, internet and phone bills, and writes off his home office. He may very well keep all of that income tax-free. That's a meaningful income for a business that takes very little time.

Tim is also able to be the only one selling Silent Bags because he has a patent. He also has a trademark, so even if someone created a quiet bag that got around his patent, they could not call it a Silent Bag because of Tim's trademark for the name brand. Thus, Tim's example shows us that even a small side gig can benefit from taking advantage of intellectual property law.

With patents and trademarks, why couldn't Tim's Silent Bags "go big" and make millions? When a side gig is run properly, it does not always "go big." Remember, many side gigs are in small markets. And selling into a small market, and only a small market, is fine. In Tim's case, there aren't enough movie or television studios that need Silent Bags to justify a business that makes thousands of products. In fact, the smallness of the market is a good thing for Tim. It keeps competitors from entering the market because they don't want to compete for a small sliver of a small pie. There is simply no way to make millions of dollars on Silent Bags. But that doesn't make it a bad idea! Tim has done quite well with his IP-based product as a side gig, even though it may never be a million dollar idea.

Let me pause for a minute and point out something that many people miss about small side gigs. Often they are as valuable as a million dollar idea. Take Tim's product. If we continue with our assumption that Tim makes $800 a month and uses write-offs to eliminate his taxes on that amount, he is generating about $10,000 per year, net. A patent term is 20 years. If Tim invests that money each year and makes an average of 7%, he will have about $500,000 at the end of the patent term. If he can go for another ten years, it's over $1 million. From that perspective, this modest patent and small side gig is worth a million dollars. You can also look at it from the standpoint of how much his income stream is worth. In fact, if Tim had $1 million in cash, he would only make

$10,000 per year in interest at most banks! Point being, don't underestimate the value of a steady income stream!

You might be asking whether it is necessary to own a patent in order to get the same value out of an idea like Tim's. The answer is that it depends on the size of the market, and the different ways that competitors can compete with other products that get around your patent. In some cases, obtaining a patent is vital. In other cases, it is helpful but not as critical. Let's talk about that in terms of Silent Bags.

The patent gives Tim the right to stop others from making silent bags. But it turns out that in the niche market of Hollywood props, there aren't any other companies that want to make silent bags. Why? The market isn't that large. The margins are not that high. In Tim's situation, the patent is a nice piece of security. It could be a good tool for protecting his market if a competitor tried to compete. But it is not necessarily a vital piece to his success.

I say this so that you can consider carefully whether or not you need a patent to execute your own great idea. If you have a real business, and you are entering a market worth $100 million, then owning a patent might be extremely important. I'm an intellectual property attorney. I love IP and love to see clients acquire patents. But if your idea is something you are going to do as a side gig to make $800 per month, then investing $10,000 (or more) in a patent may not be wise or necessary.

Of course, a patent can be the very heart of your side gig and be worth the cost and bring you 20 years of steady revenue, or even bring you millions if someone wants to buy it from you. I don't want to discourage you from getting a patent if your genius idea is patentable. In fact, you're about to see an example in which the patent was absolutely necessary because the side gig income is derived entirely from licensing the patent, and not from manufacturing a finished product at all.

Pouch Pal

I met Tim and Jen through a close friend. This young couple had a two-year-old daughter and another baby on the way. Jen had spent the past year feeding her daughter with baby food that came in pouches. The pouches, which now dominate the baby food aisle in grocery stores, were extremely convenient. Grab-and-go with a pouch. But the pouches presented a major problem as well. Kids could just squeeze it and all the food would ooze out. This would result in lost food, a messy kid, and usually food-stained furniture, car seats, or worse.

Jen put her entrepreneurial ambitions into developing a case to hold the pouches, and came to me with her idea. She and Tim had created something never-before invented, and they needed to figure out how to protect it. I joined with them in founding a company, and filed patents and trademarks all around the world. Thus, Pouch Pal was born.

This type of investment in intellectual property may not have been warranted with Tim's Silent Bags because Silent Bags are sold into a very small market. Only stage masters and property masters really need quiet bags for sound sets. But baby food pouches are sweeping the world's supermarkets, and are already a multi-billion-dollar business.

With more than a billion baby food pouches being sold each year, Jen's invention would only need to get at about one percent of the market to be a success. That would result in sales of 10,000,000 units per year. If the profit on each product is just a dollar, then the business would be a success. Thus, obtaining intellectual property protection was essential to protect Jen's idea.

This sounds like we are about to start a business, right? You should be thinking, "Wait a minute, Dana, haven't you been saying we need to start side gigs and not businesses?" If that indeed was your thought, then congrats, you are a step ahead of me. Pouch Pal had to make an important decision once it obtained the patent: Does the company raise funds from investors, source product in China, hire a sales team, and build a business? Or does the company find an existing manufacturer and license the IP to someone who is already running a business?

The choice was to license the IP, and not try to launch a company around the idea. The product was so good, and the patent and IP rights so solid, that we seriously considered launching a business. But Jen is the mother of two young kids, Tim is a successful engineer. They would have to bet the farm, and work for two to four years to build a company around Pouch Pal, and at the end of the cycle, maybe not make any money at all.

By licensing the intellectual property to someone who is *already* selling products to baby stores, Tim and Jen could take their amazing idea and turn it into a side gig. The licensee has the right to sell the product worldwide, and pays a royalty on all sales. At the same time, Tim and Jen are free to buy Pouch Pal products from the licensee and sell them on their own website and make additional cash from an online store. They make royalties from the licensee, and also make monthly revenue from selling them directly. If the licensee is successful, then Tim and Jen may make millions of dollars. Even if it is not a home run, they stand to make a steady stream of income for many years into the future, while enjoying the life they have and freedom to be with their kids when they want. They don't need to spend the next three years working long days and risking everything.

There are more than 500,000 patent applications filed each year, and less than half are issued. About 20 percent of the applications are filed by individual inventors like Jen. The rest are filed by large companies. The process of obtaining an application requires a substantial legal document, a filing fee of a few hundred dollars, and nearly three years to finally get issued.

However, with a patent in hand, many inventors can become successful entrepreneurs, or make money from their patent as a side gig.

Before you go hire an attorney to help you file a patent, start by looking at Google's patent database, http://www.google.com/patents. In order to obtain a patent, your idea must be novel and nonobvious. That means you have to look at what's been done by others in the same field. I can't tell you how often someone comes to me with a brilliant idea that has already been invented and patented.

If there's clearly no prior inventions, then it's time to sit with a patent attorney and develop your product further.

What may serve you better than a patent is a trademark, which is a much smaller investment and provides broad protection for your name, logo, or slogan. Most side gigs have a brand name or a product name, and thus trademark law is invoked. You can file a trademark on your own, or through a filing service like LegalZoom, or through trademark attorneys like me. The most important step isn't to file a trademark, but to "clear" your trademark before you launch your side gig. Rights go to the first user of a mark, so it's important that you ensure that you aren't going to infringe on someone else when you select a brand name.

When it comes to trademarks, be sure the name you choose isn't being used by someone else for similar products or services. Don't file a trademark until you've verified that there's no prior registrations or pending applications. In addition, check for unregistered users of the same or similar trademark by searching the web.

When it comes to having a "stroke of genius," remember that you are trying to build a revenue stream, not create something to spend money on. Using IP law to register and protect your idea is important, but don't lose track of the goal: to make money (not spend it). I once met a man who had spent hundreds of thousands of dollars on patents all over the world, and never actually launched his business. He really thought that by simply owning the IP he wouldn't have to do anything else. But patents and trademarks are merely tools in creating income for your business or side gig. They are not typically valuable without a plan to monetize them.

ACTION STEPS

What is your field of expertise?

- List what you are trained to do.
- List what you know how to do really well, even if you lack formal training.
- List the people who you know in your industry.
- For each person you list, also list what they do. How might they help you regarding your great idea? Are they in a position to be a customer? Do they know people who might be customers? Later, you'll interview them before you finalize your side gig launch plan.

What are your big ideas?

- List any of those strokes of genius you've had. List them all, even if you already know they aren't going to make a good side gig. I once invented the ropeless jump rope. Clearly not a big winner. I'm sure you have several ideas, from wonky to wonderful. List them all. Then work through them, one at a time looking at whether anyone else has done the same thing. Check Google Patents for similar patents (I discovered there are a half dozen ropeless jump ropes). Don't rule ideas out until you get them all down, and then go through them individually to evaluate viability. Once the list is shortened down to ideas that have not been done or patented, then start evaluating how well the idea fits into your strengths and experience. Use your list from the first exercise to help filter those ideas you generated in the second exercise. This may help you home in on that one special idea that might be worth your time and investment.

Chapter 9

You Can Be a Used [Lamborghini] Salesman!

If you've read this far, you already know I have a certain mechanical aptitude. I learned how to rebuild engines before I could drive. I taught myself a certain amount of computer programming. I've taken apart and rebuilt computers. I've built wooden book shelves and other furniture. But my aptitude for auto mechanics is probably the strongest. As a young man about to enter his twenties, it may have been one of my only strengths.

So it was no surprise when, at 19 years old, an old car caught my eye. This was in my friend's workshop, where I was doing some casual labor. I wondered why anyone would have a car just sitting on a lot collecting dust.

"What's up with that car?" I asked.

"That was my Dad's."

"Oh. Um. Is he still alive?" I asked awkwardly.

"Yeah. Oh, yeah. He's alive and well. He just sort of abandoned it here when he bought another car. He's just slow to get rid of things."

"Does it run?" I asked.

"It did when he parked it there, but it hasn't been started in a couple of years."

“Think he’d sell it to me?” I said.

“Ha.” He thought for a minute. “You’d want to buy *that*?”

“Well, if the price is right, yes,” I said. “I’d fix it up and sell it and make a little money, to be honest.”

“Let me ask him,” he replied.

It turned out that his father was happy to sell it. I paid $500 and the pink slip became mine. It needed a starter, which I replaced while it was still on the lot. I also changed the oil while I was at it. I went to Earl Scheib and got a cheap $100 paint job, and within a few weeks I had it sold for more than $2,000. For a 19-year-old kid, this was a big win! But I never turned it into a regular thing.

Nevertheless, it’s a story that demonstrates another path to a profitable side gig. Car flipping is a great side gig, particularly for those of us with mechanical aptitude.

But, what if you don’t like to work on cars? Well, if you have an aptitude for cars but not mechanics, then you still might be able to create a side gig out of car flipping. Here’s one such story.

Bill's Exotics

Bill keeps it simple. He's not a car dealer. He’s not a mechanic. He was a chiropractor by training. But he's got an instinct for the value of certain cars. And luckily for Bill, his expertise is in understanding the value of *exotic* cars. He loves Lamborghinis, Hummers and other high-priced vehicles.

He has turned his car obsession into a side gig. He'll buy an exotic car when he knows that he has absolutely gotten it for much less than it's worth. He'll then drive it, and circulate the info to exotic dealers and advertise on Craigslist. If he does it right, he can make thousands of dollars on every flip. In one transaction, he bought a Hummer for $60,000 and had a buyer the same day for $80,000.

Now, obviously, this isn't for everyone. Bill must play with a substantial sum of cash. Sometimes well over $100,000 for one car. But his return can be $10,000, $20,000 or more. If he only makes $3,000, then his return on $100,000 is 3% per month, or 36% per year. But he typically does far better. Meanwhile, Bill gets to drive some amazing cars, and he isn't working very much (or very hard) for that money. He doesn't have to own a car dealership, deal with returns, customers, liability, mechanics, and the full-time hassles that come with being "all in." He's keeping it simple, and makes his entire living from this one side gig.

I don't know all of the ins and outs of car dealing. In California, I understand that a person can sell up to five cars without a dealer's license each year. In most states it is six. Having a dealer's license is helpful, though. You can avoid paying taxes on each purchase, reducing your transactional cost and increasing your margins. Most guys like Bill don't want to own a real car dealership. So they simply partner with a small car dealer who is licensed, and then run their deals through that dealership, giving them a small fee for using their services to transact the deal.

What makes Bill's side gig awesome is that he doesn't have to fix up his cars, like I did. He just has to be sure he is buying lower than what he can sell it for. Your situation might be different, of course. You may need to do what I did when I was 19: Find a car that needs some TLC, do a little fixing, and then resell it. In the beginning, you might be flipping $1,000 cars for $1,500. But once you build up some cash and gain some experience, you might find that your sweet spot is buying for $3,000 and selling for $4,500. You may even be able to trade your way up to exotics like Bill! Or you may find that you have a mechanical problem you can fix easily, or perhaps you just know how to make a car look better cosmetically and are willing to patiently wait to sell it for a profit. You could also specialize situationally, such as looking for desperate sellers or those looking to sell quickly because they need to move.

Car flipping can be one of the best ways for a person with few skills to create a non-business. I don't mean this in an insulting way. Remember, when I did my fix-and-flip I was 19 and had few skills. If you are looking for side gig ideas and you continually find yourself saying, "But I don't know how to do such and so," or "I don't have any skills," then car flipping might be right for you.

Joanne's Car Loans

Let me tell you about a related side gig I learned from a colleague. Joanne works at a car dealership. She has for years. She's sort of an "everything" person for the dealership. She does books and accounting, deals with HR, and knows every aspect of auto sales. That's her day job and she does it well.

One day I discovered she had a side gig. What she does is buy used cars that come through the dealership that the dealership doesn't want. This situation presents itself because dealers will often accept a trade-in car even if the dealership doesn't really want it. The dealer then liquidates these cars "at wholesale" to other dealers and individuals who are car flippers. But, Joanne doesn't just flip the cars. Here's what she does: She'll buy the occasional car, *but not to flip it.* She'll buy it to sell it on financed terms. She's basically making herself a lender by buying a car, and then selling it to someone who can't pay cash. Her return for this is nearly 35% per year when you factor in the fees and interest together.

How does she do this? She works for a car dealer and buys cars from the selection of used cars on the lot. She then advertises those on Craigslist as available on a payment plan. Then she uses her knowledge to have the buyer sign loan documents and sells them the car with a lien against the title.

Obviously, she already knows the business. Good side gigs flow from doing something you are already familiar with. Joanne has the legal forms at her disposal, and she knows how the lending works for used cars. I'm sure there are also some laws that she has to comply with as a lender. But because this is her expertise, the process is easy for her.

But isn't this risky? If people don't pay, doesn't she have to spend a lot of time and money chasing them down? Is she backing tow trucks into people's driveways to repossess cars from deadbeats? Actually, no. She installs in these cars a remote GPS system with a kill switch. Not only does she know where the car is at all times, but she can kill the power and then easily go retrieve the car. However, because she has the power to do this, she never has to use it. All she has to do is send a text to the borrower and threaten to cut the power, and the borrower makes their payment right then and there through a mobile payment link.

When I met Joanne, she had 10 cars out on this type of loan. If we take an educated guess that each loan was for $5,000, then that means she had $50,000 in loans owed to her, generating over $1,500 per month in interest. In addition, for each $5,000 car she sold, she probably paid $3,000 or less. That means her investment in 10 cars may have amounted to $30,000, and in the end, she will be paid $50,000, plus five years of interest. Her $30,000 will make her about $100,000 in total return in addition to receiving her initial investment back.

How much work does Joanne need to perform each week? About an hour. It's only 10 cars. She built up to those 10 cars over a two-year period. So all she had to do was buy a car every other month, sell it and finance the purchase. Once the car is sold, payments are electronically transferred and her only hassle is when a customer fails to pay and she has to call or text them to get the payment current. She's making $1,500 per month and not even working four hours per month to earn it. It is a nice little side gig for Joanne and one that she can keep doing for years if she wants.

Should Joanne grow this into 100 cars? Probably not. That would start to — repeat after me — look like a business! Remember, a side gig is a *non*-business, not a business. She already has a day job making six figures doing something she is great at. She doesn't want to own a real dealership of her own. She doesn't want to become a car finance company. She just wants to leverage her expertise to build and maintain a side gig.

ACTION STEPS

Ask yourself the following questions:

- Could you be a used car salesman, so to speak, in the way described in this chapter?
- Do you have car aptitude? If so, write down your special skills. This might be mechanical (like me replacing a starter), or it might be industry-related, such as Joanne and her ability to buy cars cheap and then finance them for buyers.
- Are a car dummy but have the cash to buy a car? If so, then you can buy it, hold, and then sell it for a little more. You can start by combing Craigslist for opportunities. You aren't going to buy, you are going to watch. Pick a car you think is a good value and then simply watch it. How long is it listed? Does the price drop each week? You might even save the contact information so that you can ask the seller how much they sold for when the listing is dead.

- Are you a car nerd? To make money in cars, you don't have to be mechanical if you just know how to find a deal. To know how to find a deal, you need to specialize in certain models. Start narrowing in on a few makes and models you can get really familiar with, and start practicing without buying or selling. Start by watching the prices on those cars. Check Criagslist, eBay and AutoTrader for several months before you make the first purchase.

- Are you a motorcycle enthusiast? Apply the same principles as above.

Chapter 10

A Money Making Garage!

America is the land of the garage! I've traveled all over the world and can confirm that we are the Garage Capital of the World. The garage was originally intended to be a place where commuting Americans parked their cars. But I'll bet that if you have a two-car garage, it only fits one car — if that. Why? You have filled your garage with your junk. Your garage is your storage unit.

I'd like to propose that your garage become the home for your side gig. There are many things you can do with your garage other than use it to store your unused junk. One way to start is to consider selling much of that stuff to get some cash you can use to help start your side gig.

You've already learned what my parents did in their garage for side gigs. We had woodworking and stained glass tools and while both were hobbies, they were both side gigs that generated extra cash. Or perhaps for you the garage can be a place for you to comfortably fix a car you intend to flip. You might even use it to manufacture your own unique product such as Tim's Silent Bags.

Let me tell you about a great side gig that uses one-third of a three-car garage to continually create a steady flow of income for nearly 10 years running.

Cory's Audiobook Studio

Cory is a longtime friend, business partner and brilliant entrepreneur. He and I co-founded Christianaudio, now the largest Christian audiobook publisher in the world. But like most entrepreneurs, he paid his dues when he was younger. He's run a house painting franchise, done landscaping, and hustled wherever he could. We've been partners in several businesses together. But as I've already discussed, in order to be an entrepreneur and take risks, it is very useful to have a side gig. Cory's side gig came about slowly, but proved to be an important piece to his business life.

In the early years of Christianaudio, Cory needed an audiobook studio, which is something different than a typical recording studio. He read extensively on the subject and decided to build a studio in his garage. As it turns out, his little studio is so perfect for book reading that it is better than many of the high-end professional studios that charge big money.

So, not only is the "garage studio" great for our publishing business, but it also revealed itself as a great side gig opportunity. He rents it to other publishers who want to record voice-overs, audiobooks, podcasts and more. He charges a reasonable fee to let people rent his garage studio, which can total up to $500 per day. His garage turned out to be the perfect entrepreneurial double play: an awesome business asset he uses for a real business, and an ideal side gig platform.

Rather than sit there as a repository of forgotten junk, Cory's garage empowers him to continue his entrepreneurial ventures. He doesn't even have to work harder to earn this extra money. He (or his wife) often simply let people into their garage. Cory can provide a sound engineer for an additional fee (which also means someone else is there to handle the client, while Cory is doing something else). Cory can keep this mostly hands-free side gig, allow it to regularly generate money for him, and then head off to run a real business during the day. At the end of the day, he's made money merely by letting someone use his studio for the day. He has one of the best side gigs I've seen. How much does Cory make? Well, one year it was more than he made from his annual salary at his audiobook company.

I realize most of you reading this don't happen to have high-end audio sound studios in your garages. But don't miss the wider point; I know of people who rent their garage for other purposes. If you live in an area that is densely populated, your garage may have value. You might get $100, or even $200 per month to let someone use half of your garage, without any ongoing effort required on your part. You can rent your garage to a band (if you don't mind the sounds of band practice). You can build a woodshop. A relative of mine has spent years using his garage as a full-scale metalworking shop. He makes steady side gig money from metalwork and welding. What about a workshop for a product you make with a 3D printer? Or a small jewelry-making shop for those unique items you want to sell on Etsy?

At the end of the day, you can actually make your garage your side gig by renting it. Or you can look for activities to do in your garage that make money.

How to Make $100K in a Weekend

I recently realized that my storage bill had climbed to $175 a month. That meant the stuff in my storage unit was costing me $2,100 per year.

Without even connecting it at first, I realized I had an opportunity just waiting there for me. I own a fourplex that had a garage that was sitting there unrented. The reason no one wanted to rent it was because it was tandem, meaning it was long and only wide enough for one car. Since no one in my building wanted to rent it. I was simply using it to store crap I'd used to rehab items, such as wood, bags of Quikrete, some pipes, screens, etc.. I looked up garages nearby and saw that one-car garages were going for $150 to $175 a month. Okay, so maybe your light bulb just went off. But here's the thing: I'd already thought of just using that garage as *my* storage unit. But in my mind, why move all my crap to this garage for a zero-sum gain? Likewise, if I just rented the garage out for $175, it would be just to pay that same amount for my storage. Both options seemed to add up to zero. I wanted to make 1+1=3.

Instead of doing either of these, I took a weekend and built a wall to divide the garage into two parts and built a door that would access the back of the garage. I then made that back half mine. I moved my stuff into it and no longer had to pay the $175 monthly storage fee. That's $2,100 per year in my pocket. Then I rented the front half of the garage for $175 per month. All told, this equated to a net gain of $4,200 per year. And that means in 23 years, I'll have saved $100,000. But that's not really the right way to look at it. It gets even better. How? Well, if you calculate the *time-value* of money — which is the principle that money available at the present time is worth more than the same amount in the future, due to its potential earning capacity — then you make $100,000 in far *less* than 23 years. When you factor in the time-value of money, this move is now actually worth $100,000 *within 15 years*. Not only that, but when you consider that these numbers would increase with inflation, that $100,000 gain is achieved in less than 10 years.

Do you get it? I made a decision to inconvenience a single weekend and spent a little money on two-by-fours and drywall, and it changed my next decade of earning by $100,000. Now while you may not have an empty garage at an apartment complex you own (yet), take a moment and consider the value of something you can do to save a couple hundred bucks a month, and then the small changes you can make to *add* a few hundred bucks a month. Think about what that could mean for your life. Those things add up to real money over a fairly short period of time.

Here's another thing I did this year. I just killed my lavish fitness club membership ($140/month) in favor of a YMCA membership. That's a net gain of $100 a month. I also just joined a food delivery service that's going to save me $200 per month on groceries because I consistently overbuy and end up not even using much of what I pay for. That's a $300/month gain and amounts to $3,600 a year in savings. If you again do the time-value math, you'll see that it equates to $87,000 in just 15 years.

But wait! Maybe you've read my book *Opt Out*, or some of my articles. You know I'm not an advocate of trying to penny pinch, or living on a tight budget. It might sound like I'm telling you to be cheap. I'm not. I don't want you to be cheap or live on a budget. The goal of my story is to get you to think differently about money, particularly large, recurring monthly expenses. These have massive long-term value. Look at money differently, and understand the long-term cost of allowing unnecessary recurring expenses to hurt your future success.

Here's an example of what you might do. Cut the cable bill by killing Cox or Time Warner (or whoever your regional provider is) and buy YouTube TV for $35 a month. I have it and love it. I use it at my vacation condo for free, and my daughter gets to use it for free, too. That's a savings of $100 a month.

What I don't want you to do is be cheap. Don't tip 15% and think you are really adding value to your present or future success. If you eat out like I do (and hopefully you don't!), you'll be spending $1,000 a month on restaurant tabs. Tipping at that level amounts to $200. If I try to cut my favorite bartender down by a bit, I'll save $50 a month … but I'll also get no favors from Eddie at the bar, either. It would hurt my reputation and friendships, and it would make me into a cheapo tightwad who will never get a last-minute table on a busy night. Don't ask your friends to use a calculator to divide the dinner bill. Just split it equally, even if you had one less drink than the others. Chill and enjoy your friends. Be generous. Don't be "that" *guy*. Those small amounts never add up to the true cost of being cheap.

Instead, go find a couple of ways to make $100,000 in one weekend and then toast your success with a drink at your favorite bar ... and then tip more than you should!

Office Manager Turned Jewelry Maker

Kylie Watts is an office manager in Maine, a state where lobster is a major industry. In the lobster business, there's a regulation about how long a lobster's body must be in order to be a fair catch. Specimens measuring less than 3.25 inches, or more than 5 inches, go back into the water. The industry has a gauge to measure this; typically a brass measuring stick.

Kylie started taking those brass instruments and bending them into bracelet cuffs. The product was a hit, and she was featured in an article at Inc. online. She called it the Perfect Catch Cuff and, as you can imagine, people loved the idea of putting a cuff on their "perfect catch."

Kylie's business originally was run from inside her home. But she moved things into her garden shed when production got too messy. Kylie is a great example of the rise in the American garage brand (or in this case, a woodshed brand!). Your garage, garden shed, basement or attic is waiting for you to join the ranks of people making money with side gigs; and no commute required.

The Bottle Factory

My friend Eric has a normal day job as a banker. While Eric's job is certainly more demanding than the stereotype we associate with the phrase "banker's hours," I can tell you that there's a real advantage to having a job that you can truly leave behind when you leave the office. Not everyone has an office job that doesn't follow them home with work of some kind.

If you have a day job that doesn't go home with you each night, then a side gig can be the perfect complement. Here's how it worked with Eric: Starting as a small hobby, he took empty beer and wine bottles and used some cutting tools to make them into glasses, vases, candle holders and such. It grew into a business called San Diego Bottle Factory. The garage *is* the factory.

Eric's bottle factory gives him a side gig he can do after his day job is done. He collects bottles from various sources, cuts them into drinking glasses, vases or candle holders, cleans them up and then sells them online. He uses social media to post each new set of products.

In addition to bottles, Eric makes coasters from the cardboard beer cases. The base for the coasters consists of a flat ceramic product, onto which Eric laminates beer labels so that his customers can buy branded beer coasters made of repurposed and recycled materials. Eric's business is green in two ways: He is upcycling glass that might be thrown away, and he's making greenbacks along the way! (Sorry, I couldn't resist; there's a jingle waiting to be written in there somewhere.)

Eric's non-business required very little initial investment. Remember, that's part of what makes the perfect side gig. The bottle factory doesn't require much time from Eric, so he's not distracted from his day job. There's no need for ongoing financial investment to keep the bottle factory going. His side gig is low risk, low stress and makes extra money that he can use to save for retirement, or just to buy more beer if that's what he wants!

ACTION STEPS

Garage Brainstorming

Go sit in your garage and think. Some people call this meditation. I call it "garage time." It's pretty much the same thing, but garage time might also include an ice cold bottle of craft beer in your hand. Sit in that old recliner that you've been meaning to throw away and let your mind wander. Look around your garage and visualize it as a space that makes you money. See it as a workshop, organized and well-lit. See it as a source for your creativity. See it as a factory. See your garage as a place someone pays you rent for, every month while you do nothing.

Write down your feelings after your garage meditation session. Write down any ideas you have. Write down words that come to your mind. Even simply writing, "my factory" is useful as part of this exercise. Don't judge at this point. Don't rule out things you might do with your garage. Just think of possibilities and log those. We'll come back to this later.

Chapter 11

Domain Names

My business partner Nate buys domain names. He's got a couple of different angles to this that I'd like to share with you because most of the ways he uses domain names are very passive, and they generate meaningful cash.

Think of domain names as a sort of "real estate" on the Internet. Like land that hasn't been developed, some domains have big value and others have low value, and many in between have underutilized value.

Your job is to seek opportunity in that "twilight zone" between low and high value domains. You do this by looking for ways to take an unused domain and position it to gain value.

Sometimes this is simply done by finding domain names that are cheap and selling them for more. I once registered several "LLC" domains for a business venture, and when I was done, I didn't need most of them. I put them on an auction site and sold a couple of them. One in particular was llcfile.com, which I paid $10 for, and sold for $750.

But there's another path that could make for an even better side gig than merely buying and reselling domains. Nate calls it "rank and rent."

Here's how it works. You actually don't start with a domain name. You start with finding a keyword search string that's relevant to a specific geographic market, and a related specific product or service. You might even start with your own town, and a subject you don't mind writing about. Are you a foodie? Write about catering in your town. Do some searches and see what you get when you search for "catering in Austin" or "party catering in Riverside." See what comes up. It's probably businesses that provide catering in your town.

Now take that subject and that city name and buy a relevant domain name, e.g. partycateringriverside.com. Then, build a simple WordPress site with long articles on the subject of party catering services in Riverside. The website may take a year to rank. But during that year you can accelerate the ranking by writing other articles for third-party websites that have links back to *your* website. And embedded in those articles you write are relevant keywords that improve your ranking. When your site finally ranks on page one of the Google search results, you can offer to rent it to someone who does catering in Riverside. Nate has done this several times and generally commands $500 per month for each site. The rental income can last for years. Or eventually you might just sell the site for $10,000 to someone who really wants to have a highly ranked website.

You didn't have to start a catering business, and now you potentially have $500 in passive income every month. Do that ten times and in a year or two, you may not need your day job.

The key is that if you niche down far enough, you don't have to build a big, deep website. It all comes down to the vertical, the keyword, the domain. Most of my domaining is done with smaller niche domains. Something like sandiegoexterminator.com. Google loves content that is unique, topical and complete. Google loves links, which is what feeds the Google beast.

Creating content doesn't have to be a daunting or intimidating task. Sure, it can take a few hours per article, but you may only need a dozen articles on your site, and another dozen that you put out there onto other blogs. You can do it yourself, or pay a professional writer to do it for you from a freelancing site like Upwork for a smaller fee than you might guess.

You can even pay to have your articles placed on third-party sites so that you don't have to spend your time looking for places to post your outside articles.

Want a pro hack? Use AnswerThePublic.com to evaluate the keywords you might choose to deploy.

The game you are playing here is called SEO, or "search engine optimization." That means you are writing content in a way that optimizes how Google and other search engines see and rank your content.

The cool part about doing this type of side gig is that you also develop a skill you can sell or use for other businesses. People will pay YOU to write their articles if you know the game. They'll partner with you in business. They'll look to consult with you for paid advice.

Of course, this chapter can't be an exhaustive lesson on SEO, but there are a ton of resources on the subject. I won't get deep into it here. If this is your jam, get out there and take some SEO courses, learn to write for the search engines algorithm, and hone those skills to make the easiest passive income you can imagine.

Chapter 12

That Easy Thing That No One Else Wants to Do

It may seem obvious, but there are a variety of tasks that people just don't want to do. No matter how easy it is, people just don't want to do it themselves. This includes personal tasks as well as business tasks. If you are trying to figure out your side gig, you might consider looking at things people don't want to do themselves.

The Sunday Night Fax

I have a friend who is semi-retired. He was a serial entrepreneur for most of his life. But in his later years, Hank has scaled back his entrepreneurial activity and spent more of his time playing golf. He loves the sport and is out on the links at least twice a week.

Playing golf twice a week can be quite expensive. Greens fees of $100 are common in California, particularly if you want to use a golf cart (some courses require them). Which means if you want to play twice a week, you'd better budget $800 per month for golf.

A satisfying side gig doesn't necessarily have to generate cash flow; sometimes it's enough if it simply offsets a significant cost you would otherwise incur. In other words, Hank doesn't need to earn $800 per month from one of his investments if he can just find a way to golf for free, right? Well, that's exactly what he did.

Here's how that happened. Many years ago, Hank found a software program that would auto-fax to a list of recipients. He used it for one of his own businesses for years. He could send out an updated price list at any given time with the click of a mouse, and all of his customers would instantly receive his updated prices. It was a great business tool before email took over.

Someone at his local golf course mentioned how they needed to tell their members about the weekly golf special. After some discussion, Hank learned the golf course wanted to send a fax of the weekly specials and other information every Sunday to a list of players who had signed up for the fax alerts.

It seemed complicated and too much work for the golf course folks. So he offered to take care of this task for them in exchange for free golf. For Hank, it would amount to an hour every Sunday night, but otherwise didn't cost him anything. And the golf course avoided the need to buy software, let alone hire an outside firm to perform this service.

So let's examine this, because this story has lessons that go far beyond golf and is not wedded to any one technology. Giving my friend free golf really didn't cost the course anything, which made this a complete win-win: zero cost on both ends but saving each party hundreds of dollars every month. An outside service might have cost the golf course $100 per week. And of course this nifty little side gig gave Hank a tax-free value of $800 per month even if he only plays golf twice a week. *The value of this side gig actually goes UP the more he plays golf!* How great is that?

Why wouldn't the golf course simply handle this internally? It seems like an easy task, right? Well, it goes back to my original statement at the outset of this chapter: There are just some things in life or business that people don't want to do. Because it doesn't really cost them anything, it's completely understandable why the course staff would rather hand this off to Hank in exchange for free golf.

Hank has kept that side gig for many years, even as email replaced the fax machine. (He now sends the information automatically by email.) I doubt that there is any tax consequence for this deal, either. Imagine having $800 in tax-free income that you could apply to something you loved, like golf. If you had to earn enough to pay for this with after-tax income, the cost would probably be closer to $1,300 per month.

Hank is not a technology expert. He has no unique skills when it comes to faxing or emailing. He simply has found an opportunity to do something that others felt was unpleasant or challenging. This might be an important key for you to embrace. If you feel that you lack a skill or expertise, you should realize that you don't necessarily need any special training or education to have a side gig. You can find opportunities where others are too lazy or too ambivalent to do it themselves. We'll discuss other examples later, but first let me tell you about another person doing a side gig that capitalized on this same dynamic.

Jennifer's Social Media Management

There's one thing that many small businesses *want* to do, but can't find the time or energy to execute on their own: social media. Companies run by people over the age of 50 are unlikely to have the desire or understanding to handle a company's social media presence. But all company owners *wish* that their company had that large, all-important social media footprint.

Businesses today not only need to have a presence on social media (such as Facebook, Instagram, Twitter, etc.), but they also need to actively *engage* their customers there. For a typical small business, this requires a staff person who not only understands the company well but also is adept at engaging audiences through social media. It turns out this is hard to find. Why? Well, those who know social media tend to be young ... very young. And what you generally don't get with a young employee is maturity and an understanding of how to blend a company's existing messaging with new media.

Sure, there are large agencies that perform this type of task. They don't come cheap, however. Since small businesses make up the majority of commerce in the U.S., this represents a great opportunity for the right person. That's because not only are most businesses too small to justify hiring a large outside agency, but even if they *did* they'd still need to find a staff person willing and able to interface between the company and agency.

The result is a strategic window for those who can create their own non-business in managing social media for small companies. Here's one story of a woman who does just that.

Jennifer is a young, hard-working entrepreneur. She is working diligently to launch her main business. But to help ensure that she pays her bills each month, she does something that she is good at, and that others are not: social media. She's a millennial. She's been raised on social media. She knows how to use Snapchat. She can do this in her sleep. So, to exploit her talent and bring in steady income, she manages social media accounts for several small companies.

For $200 per month, Jennifer will handle a company's social online presence. She'll ensure that posts appear at least weekly across all social media platforms. She uses software that gives her a dashboard so that she can track each of her client's social media activity. She can even load up many posts in one shot and then let the software auto-post it while she sleeps. She manages five companies in just a few hours per week. That earns her $1,000 per month with minimal disruption from her main business focus.

If Jennifer had a day job, she could rake in $1,000 per month from her side gig and save thousands of dollars per year, while also giving herself extra cash to build a better future. She could use that money to offset the mortgage on a condo or house.

What Jennifer has done is create an efficient way to do something that others don't want to learn how to do. Remember the win-win arrangement I described with Hank's Sunday night golf fax? The golf course is perfectly happy, and so is Hank. Similarly, with Jennifer's business, the small company feels like they are getting a steal. They don't have to mess with Facebook, Instagram, Tumblr, Snapchat, TikTok, or LinkedIn. For one small fee, they ensure that their company has an adequate presence on these platforms. And Jennifer gets to do something that is quick and easy for her, empowered by time-saving software, and she can make almost as much as if she worked a full-time minimum wage job. This gives her the ability to keep putting her time into her main business venture.

The Virtual Assistant

Jessica is a mother of three, which makes her a busy chauffeur most days. But she is not a frazzled mom, by any means. She's a militant time manager, and highly organized. Before having a family to manage, she was an executive assistant and she was damned good at it, too. She managed the busy schedules of executives, handling everything from business communications to picking up the dry cleaning. She could plan events, manage projects, deal with people at all levels, and keep her employer on track and productive.

When she wanted to start making money with a side gig, she decided to do what she was good at, but not at an office. She became a virtual assistant. She started by offering her services on elance.com (now Upwork.com), and now has a steady stream of work that she can do from home or even from her car in between pick-ups and drop-offs at her kids' soccer practice. Some of her clients are distant and she manages everything through email and project management software provided by her employer. Other clients are local; she'll even run errands for them while she is already doing them for herself.

Her side gig provides her a substantial monthly income, but also gives her a sense of being in business, and doing what she is good at. And she gets to do all this without sitting at a desk in an office building! She maintains her freedom while earning nearly the same income she would have gotten at a full-time job.

Other Unpleasant Jobs

I once met a young man in the supermarket who was shopping for an elderly woman. The woman was well off, and paid the man handsomely for shopping and running errands.

I know of someone whose side gig is to replace propane tanks on gas barbecues at vacation condos. He charges a flat fee for the service that he feels is fair and profitable. The property owners feel like they are getting a deal because paying a fixed fee to swap out tanks on the grill is far cheaper than paying a handyman to do the work. It's one less thing they have to worry about.

I've owned property management companies in the past. In that capacity, I've hired many individuals for unpleasant tasks:

cleaning ceiling fans, checking on televisions, replacing batteries in remote controls, even the simple task of meeting someone at a rental unit to let them in. These are tasks that can be done by a person with little or no training, and the income can add up quickly for anyone willing to hustle and do the things that no one else wants to do. In fact, I know of one individual who clears toilet drains for property management companies. Is it pleasant work? Nope. But that's why it's a highly in-demand service … and an opportunity for anyone willing to help management companies save on expensive but unnecessary plumbing calls.

We'll talk later about platforms that allow anyone to earn money as a driver, such as Uber and Lyft. You already know about those. But did you know that similar opportunities exist for delivering packages? Or the buying (and delivering) of groceries? Or even picking up and bringing to your doorstep something you purchased on Craigslist? There are many new platforms that provide a means to match the customer with the "picker upper," and each handles payment and security smoothly.

ACTION STEPS

- Ask yourself: What can I do that someone else doesn't want to do? Sit down and make a list of things, however unpleasant, that someone else might not want to do. Try to list 100 things.

- Next, brainstorm opportunities around your list.
- Next, add the names of people you might know who could use one of the services on your list. Call or email those people and ask. But do not propose that you do these things for them! Instead, tell them you are reading a book about side gigs and your homework is to find people who "might" use a certain type of service, and then ask them if they currently use anyone for such things, or if they would be willing to. Write down and keep track of their responses, as it will be part of what we use to help narrow your eventual list of side gigs.

Chapter 13

Royalties and Recurring Revenue

Have you ever met someone who had a great idea, and you wish you could do something to piggyback on what *they* are doing? For instance, let's say your neighbor is an inventor who shows you his new machine for water purification ... and your brother-in-law happens to be an executive at a big company that is in the business of water purification. You introduce them and bam, the neighbor is driving a new car and looking slightly richer than before. The million-dollar question, of course, is: *How do you get a piece of that action?*

Well, it can be easy to do in some cases. The key is spotting a feasible opportunity, and then trying to make yourself valuable. Of course, in some cases it just won't be feasible and you'll have to chalk up your matchmaking efforts as a "nice try" founded in goodwill and a desire to help others.

But let's say you *do* find a feasible opportunity. You want to put yourself into the middle of a deal and make a fee, right? The reality is that sometimes it works, and sometimes it doesn't. When does it *not* work? Well, in many businesses, the parties who get paid a commission are required to have a particular license. Realtors cannot share their fees, for example. Even if you bring a new client who buys a house and makes the real estate agent $10,000, you cannot share in that commission unless you get a real estate license. Attorneys may not share fees either. As an attorney, if you send me a client, I will do my best to show appreciation. I may buy you lunch. I may reciprocate by sending *you* a client or contact. I may even give you some advice without billing you. But I cannot share the fee.

Simply put, it isn't feasible to share a fee with licensed professionals when you aren't also licensed.

However, there actually is a class of businesspeople who charge a fee for making introductions. We typically refer to them as "agents." The word agent is a broad term that refers to anyone who has the authority of a principal to act on the principal's behalf. An agent can be anyone with an agreement to act on someone's behalf. In the real world, it is not common for a person to grant agency to someone. You have probably never given someone true authority to act on your behalf, except maybe when you have hired a REALTOR ® to be your agent.

So, what other types of agents are out there? Well, if you write a book, you may enlist a book agent. If you're an actor, you hire an agent to find you work. Agents can charge a fee for something as simple as an introduction.

While most agents are working under some kind of license, not all types of agency relationships require a special license. Let me tell you about one agent who has created side gig income from putting deals together.

Stan is a project manager. His talents have given him the reputation as the "go-to guy." One day he started working with a publishing company that was looking for authors to handle short educational pieces. They knew Stan would have many contacts. However, Stan wanted to do more than make mere introductions. He knew that introductions alone would not put anything in his pocket. He also knew that such introductions have real value. The publisher, after all, would get access to terrific content providers, and the authors would receive ongoing income. There's clear value on both ends. And if he looked at introductions like everyone else does, as if it's just a routine favor undeserving of anything more than a verbal thank you, then he would probably receive nothing for his introduction.

So he did something you've seen me advocate repeatedly throughout this book: He thought outside the box, got creative, and took action. He asked the publisher to let him step in as an agent for the authors he procured. They liked the idea because it would make their job even easier. Stan would do all of the legwork, vet the authors, and bring the best of the best to the table. The cost to the publisher was the same, and the authors would share their cut with Stan.

Stan didn't need a contract with the publisher to do this, but he had a clear understanding that the writers he secured would be "his" and that the publisher would not go around him. He had a one-page agreement with his authors that made him their "agent" for purposes of this publisher only. His fee for this was 15% of whatever the author made from the deals with that publisher.

Stan started approaching promising candidates and put several authors in front of the publisher. He signed them up, and the publisher picked a few of them to proceed. Stan was not a formal publishing agent. He wasn't in the publishing business. He just happened to find a publisher who trusted him, and he located authors who were open to new channels to publish their content.

How well did this little non-business do for Stan? Well, in the first year alone, his authors collected more than $10,000 in publisher payments. That meant $1,500 to Stan, and the income didn't stop there. As those authors received new projects from the publisher, Stan gets paid on those as well. A year later, Stan had tripled his income. That's $4,500 per year, and growing. A perfect side gig, making nearly $400 per month and increasing over time.

What does Stan have to do to earn this side income? Nothing, once he has signed up his author! He has no ongoing responsibilities. Thus, Stan gets $400 every month, and he doesn't have to work one hour per week, or even one hour per month. He has a royalty stream that will keep paying him for many years, maybe for his entire life.

What is the value of a lifetime stream of revenue? If you want to receive $400 per month in income, you would have to put about $100,000 in the bank at 5%. Banks don't pay that well today. In fact, finding even 2% interest is difficult. Thus, you might be able to generate $400 per month if you deposit about $200,000 in the bank and simply let it collect interest. Thus, the value of this income stream to Stan is the same as if he had put $200,000 in the bank. That's the great part about a side gig. You can create consistent revenue every month with almost no cash, and the net effect is the same as if you had hundreds of thousands of dollars in the bank. That's the value of your side gig.

Likewise, if you put $400 per month into an index fund that performs mildly well, you could have a million dollars by the time you retire. One might say that Stan basically set up a million dollar deal when he locked down his $400/month commission. It may not seem like much when you view the monthly increments. But, that monthly $400, if properly used, will be life changing for Stan.

For very little effort, Stan created a win-win-win in which he makes perpetual money, his publisher friends make money, and his author friends make money.

As we have seen with other side gigs, Stan's business might not be viable if it was run as a "real" business. Stan needs to make a good salary to live. So for him to grow the agency into a full-time gig, he would have to work a lot more hours, manage many publishers and authors, and have all of the ups and downs of a typical business. As a side gig, however, the model is perfect. But as a real business, it would not have the same simplicity and freedom.

Placing yourself into the middle of a deal can often create a delicate balancing act. You risk ruining friendships and relationships. Choose wisely when you decide to make this kind of deal happen.

The great thing is, some short-term deals can still bring a tidy little pile of cash. One example that sticks out in my mind was a woman named Rose. Rose knew someone who knew someone. I'm not kidding, it was that removed. Rose didn't have the actual contacts that a company needed. But she knew the person who did. Typically, this type of deal doesn't play out very well. Why should Rose get paid for making an introduction, when the introduction was to someone else who would be making an introduction?

However, it worked out in this case because the introduction was not just to a random friend. It was with an experienced sales rep. And that rep had a black book full of important contacts. So it was no surprise that this person could become a key to the success of any company that used the rep.

Here's how it played out. Rose's contact knew the rep, and so made the introduction and asked for a fee. The company was hesitant at first, but then made her an offer. They would not give her a fee based on what the company sold. Instead, the company would pay her a fee based on what the *sales rep* would make. That way, if the sales rep was terrible there would be little or no ongoing obligation to the original introducer or Rose. If the sales rep was awesome, then there would be a small percentage of revenue paid to Rose and the introducer for the introduction. In addition, if the sales rep quit, or was fired, there would be no ongoing payments to anyone. The deal turned out to be a win-win.

However, one part of this arrangement is worth noting — the woman who made the original introduction thought she would get rich from this introduction. That didn't happen. And in the world of business, it *shouldn't* happen. No wise business will give away millions to the person who simply introduced them to a sales rep.

How did it play out? Well, the sales rep got a deal to make 10 percent of the sales she made through her network. This is a typical sales rep commission. Then the company agreed to pay 10 percent of what they paid the sales rep to the introducer. That's 10 percent of the rep's 10 percent. That equals 1 percent of the total sales made by the rep. If the rep sells $10 million per year of product, then the rep earns a $100,000 commission per year for her work. That means the introducer gets 10 percent of that, or in this case, $10,000 per year.

In my opinion, the introducer landed an incredible deal. Imagine making $10,000 per year for doing nothing but having made an introduction. It worked for this introducer. While her dreams of striking it rich were dashed, no one could doubt that she made a substantial sum.

Making commissions from putting deals together is not the only way to create passive income as a side gig. I'll tell you a true story about a side gig I tried to buy. I failed to get the deal, but it is a good example of the kind of deals out there if you are willing to go hunting.

Audio Rights and Royalties

As you know from reading this book, I co-founded a successful audiobook business more than 15 years ago. Some years back, I became aware that a much larger audiobook company had gone bankrupt. Although the assets of the bankruptcy estate were not right for our publishing business, I decided it would be prudent for me to stay up to date on the bankruptcy.

Toward the end of the bankruptcy, the court had sold most of the company's assets and was using that to pay creditors. But after selling almost everything the court realized it had not yet sold off several hundred audio recordings. These recordings were being used by Amazon's Audible service, as well as several other large distributors, even during bankruptcy.

The recordings had a legal problem: The bankruptcy court had the right to sell the recordings, but all of the licenses from the publishers had been terminated. If I purchased these recordings out of bankruptcy, I would need to go back to each publisher and ask them to renegotiate a deal to allow me to start selling them again. That would be a royal pain, and if a publisher said "No" I would own an audio recording that I could not use.

However, there was one little-known perk that would come with the purchase of these audio rights. The ongoing sales by

Audible and other distributors during bankruptcy were being held in trust for the eventual buyer of the assets. If you could somehow buy these assets from the bankruptcy court, you would have the right to collect all of the money that was just sitting there waiting to be paid.

Unfortunately, I was not the only one who knew this. Someone else did as well.

I went to the bankruptcy court on the day of bidding. I bid against the other bidder. At one point, I reached my financial limit and dropped out. The other bidder won. I can't tell you precisely what the bidder did ultimately with the assets, but here's what the deal would have looked like if I had won.

My target purchase price was $40,000. The amount sitting in third-party accounts just waiting to be collected was at least $40,000. So I would have recouped all of my money immediately after purchasing the rights. The annual income from the assets was about $30,000, and climbing each year. Thus, if I had won, I would have collected $40,000 immediately, and then collected $30,000 per year for doing nothing but simply owning the rights. The hitch was that I would have needed to renegotiate the rights with the underlying publishers and authors, and that was just too risky for me. In retrospect, I should have bid more and tried to win the auction. Why? Because that income on audiobook royalties has steadily increased since then. The $30,000 in annual income is now probably more than $70,000 per year and climbing!

But alas, the other bidder had more cash. They bid over $100,000 and I had dropped out of the bidding. At the time, I had that amount of cash, but wasn't willing to put that much at risk, given the circumstances. The other party was willing to take the risk, and they probably made their investment back within three years or less. This is a side gig that I missed out on because I couldn't bid high enough. If I had the risk tolerance at the time and had bid well over $100,000, then I could have recouped my investment within a few years and simply continued cashing checks after that.

This type of deal is not for everyone. First, you might not have the money to bid on these kinds of bankruptcy asset sales. Second, even if you do have the money, if you don't know the business very well you'll be taking on added risk. I happened to know this particular business because I own part of a publishing company. My expertise diminished the risk. If you do something like this, be sure it is in your realm of expertise. Perform your due diligence. Be sure you are confident in what you can do with the assets. But just know that buying royalties can change your life, and produce income that lasts for decades.

Here's another example of someone finding ongoing revenue from bankruptcy assets.

Golf Cart GPS Units

Robert is a wily old codger. He's been an entrepreneur his entire life. He's funny. He's brash. And he's not afraid to take some risks occasionally. I met him through one of my clients, and had a beer with him one day.

He made a joke about how his wife was bugging him to make more money so she could spend it. He laughed and then said, "I'm just kidding. I'm damn lucky she's put up with me this long."

We sipped our beer at a brewery near my office. I wanted to know how he managed to live the great life he had while seemingly not working at all. So I asked him and he laughed.

"All right, I'll tell you my secret. It's complicated, but I'll tell you."

He proceeded to explain that he had spent much of his career in the golf business. In fact, he had been an early pioneer in the field of golf cart display units. I'm referring to the visual display console in golf carts that shows a golfer his location on a green, distance to the pin, and other useful information.

One day Robert heard that another company in the golf space had declared bankruptcy. The company was being liquidated by a court and the creditors were being paid from the proceeds of the liquidated assets. It was a small company, so there were not many parties interested in the assets.

Robert decided to look into it. He learned that the company had two main assets. One was software technology that connected GPS to the display screens mounted on golf carts. The other asset resided in the fact that the company owned the display screens mounted on golf carts at dozens of golf courses. Stick with me here. Basically, the bankruptcy court was selling some software and display screens.

Robert decided to bid on the assets. He won. He then took the software technology and found a larger company in the same business and sold them the bucket of assets that included the technology. He didn't want to run a software business. So he simply pocketed a profit on the sale of the technology.

Robert's eye was on bigger game: those display screens. The assets he *didn't* sell were approximately 1,000 monitors mounted to golf carts all over the Midwest.

Now if you had asked me, a know-it-all IP attorney, I might have told Robert to keep the intellectual property and sell the monitors. Who wants to own a bunch of outdated monitors sitting at golf courses across several states? Well, Robert knew better than me. He wasn't looking for a business. He was looking for a *non*-business. He wanted side gig income, not another business to run.

So let's recap what's happened so far. The sale of the technology to the large company paid Robert back for what he paid the bankruptcy court, and made him a profit. But now he owned 1,000 monitors mounted to golf carts. What did this mean exactly?

Well, those monitors were being *leased* to the golf courses. At the time we had a beer, he was making $40,000 per month in lease payments for those monitors. Every month, month after month, Robert collected serious money from every golf course for those monitors.

He bought a business. He sold the business. But then kept the non-business piece so he could enjoy the side gig without the hassle of the "real" business.

But you might ask, "Doesn't Robert have to run a business to keep up with those monitors?" Yes, the income is not completely passive. It does involve some work. For instance, when a monitor breaks, he has to replace it. He had a source for even better monitors that cost only a few hundred dollars each. He would simply ship the golf course a new monitor when one broke, and let them pull off the old one, trash it, and mount the new one. When it's all said and done, Robert doesn't have to work very much to earn that $40,000 per month. It doesn't require a full-time commitment; there is no office, and there are no employees.

Sure, he could try to turn it into a business. But why? To put large sums of money at risk, work 80-hour weeks, all in the hopes of building a multi-million-dollar business? No thanks. Robert lived a very good life on his $40,000 per month.

Bankruptcy court is not the only place to acquire money-making assets. I once bid on assets from a large auction house that only handled intellectual property. I was interested in buying a large volume of videos. The auction was for digital media, and most of it existed as older, physical media, such as CDs, DVDs, etc. I'm glad I didn't end up closing on this purchase — turned out to be four full-sized shipping containers of physical media!

Bidding to buy IP can be done in bankruptcy court, but it can also be done by approaching the winning bidder in bankruptcy. What if the winner wants to sell part of what they bought? Moreover, the winning bidder is often a creditor or bank. Banks don't want to own business assets. So if they win the assets in a bankruptcy auction, they might be willing to sell them at a reasonable price just to get cash and dump the assets.

If you want to look into this further, Ocean Tomo handles IP auctions (http://www.oceantomo.com). Copyright royalties are sold on Royalty Exchange (http://www.royaltyexchange.com). There are also patent brokerages, such as ICAP (http://icappatentbrokerage.com/).

But remember that if you want a side gig, you don't want to just buy a piece of paper. You don't want to just buy a patent. *You want to buy IP that is tied to an income stream.* So if you bid for IP rights, be sure you are buying ongoing royalties, and not just a patent registration.

Other than auctions and bankruptcy, royalties and ongoing revenue can also be found by shopping for side gigs that are web-based. Websites can be found on Flippa, as I discussed earlier. But, if you want to shop for something beyond just a web business, check out BizBuySell.com and MergerNetwork. Both of these platforms list credible, income-producing businesses for sale. You should be wary of deals that make aggressive claims about income, or that simply have prices that are out of your reach. Use the exercises at the end of this chapter to begin watching businesses on these sites.

You can also consider creating royalty income from scratch. There are many ways to do this. For now, let me give you one example that worked for someone I know.

The Ebook Mogul

Have you ever downloaded one of the great American classics on ebook? Henry James or Steinbeck, perhaps? You'll see that most of the downloads are not free. These books are in the public domain, but you will still usually pay at least 99 cents for an ebook. Why? Because a publisher has put time and money into formatting, editing, writing a foreword, and developing book cover art.

I know of someone who does this on his own. He basically became a public domain ebook publisher. He took hundreds of books and reformatted them into a clean digital format. He had cover designs created for each book and added forewords of his own. He worked on writing good summaries and descriptions for the bookstore listings. He then put the ebooks into marketplaces on Amazon, Google and Apple. He thought, "Why not do what other publishers are doing, and try to do it a little better?"

Within a year of doing this he was making over $2,000 per month in revenue. Once the books were done and loaded, he had no other ongoing obligations.

Now you might be thinking you could do the same. I would advise against it. That's because making revisions is quite time consuming, not to mention formatting and cover creation. You can also expect ferocious competition. However, you *can* construct your own side gig in this space by creating *your own ebook* using new, unique content.

I know of fiction authors who directly publish their works on Amazon and make $4,000 per month. They don't have agents. They don't have an official publisher. They wrote their novels and now earn more than most traditionally published authors. They experience deep fulfillment and are also nicely compensated.

You can also do well with non-fiction. Do you have something useful and unique to say? If so, consider creating an ebook. I bought an informational ebook before moving to Bali for my sabbatical. I paid $9.99 directly to the author to learn how expats live in Bali. The ebook was worth every penny. The key is to write useful content in a niche that is unique to you. Have you been through a particular medical issue or surgery? Write an ebook to help others, and you can make ongoing income to boot. Or create a guide to a place you know well and sell it to travelers, who would love to know the details of your favorite city or village.

You can also make videos out of your expertise and experience. YouTube shares revenue with video creators. If you produce videos that people actually want to watch, you can automatically generate ongoing revenue from them. Consider the topics you know well and whether you can put that knowledge and experience into an ebook or video, and use that to create side gig revenue that could last for years.

ACTION STEPS

Watch and Learn

- Create an account on BizBuySell.com and MergerNetwork.com. Conduct searches that are in your geographic area once per week, and start tracking any listing that is under $100,000. Exclude franchises, business opportunities, or businesses with no existing income. The goal is to find companies that are suffering, distressed, or in some way broken but fixable. You aren't going to buy any of these; you are simply going to watch them and learn. You want to see if the price drops, or if the business sells. You want to watch for how long a listing is live. You want to see enough opportunities so that you develop a sense of what a good deal might look like. You learn this by watching the market over time.
- After three months, take what you've learned and look for patterns. What types of businesses did you see that had high income and a low purchase price? What type of businesses appear the most? These may be the very type of business *not* to buy. You may notice an

occasional rare business that is inexpensive and has solid income. Those are the kind of businesses you'll want to look into further.

- Browse the sites above as well as Ocean Tomo and any other site that sells royalties and IP, such as Royalty Exchange. Look for IP that has existing income and start asking questions. Remember, your job at this stage is to research only. Watch and learn.

Chapter 14

Selling Your Time

What's your time worth?

One of the big challenges with picking a side gig is assessing the opportunity based on how much you currently earn for your time.

And since each of us is at a different station in life, that makes our answers vary widely.

As an attorney and entrepreneur, my time is worth over $500 per hour as of 2020. That means if I have a side gig that consumes two hours per week and brings in $1,000 per month, then I'm screwed. That's because I could normally make $4,000 with those same hours. That particular side gig would be a bad investment of my time.

But let's say you're just starting out and you make $12 per hour at your job ... that means a side gig earning you $1,000 per month for eight hours of work would mean your time-for-pay is $125 per hour.

That's ***10 times*** your hourly pay. That's a kick-ass side gig!

Or let's look at a level in between the two previous examples. Let's say you earn $5,000 per month at your job based on a 40-hour work week. That comes out to $31.25 per hour. In this case, a side gig that brings in $1,000 per month for two hours per week (which equates to $125/hour) is still ***more than three times*** your current rate. That's exciting and clearly a good use of your time.

Simply put, you want a side gig that's properly correlated to your hourly value so that you don't waste your time just to make less.

Let's give you another example.

My dad was a phone man for AT&T. He made time and a half for extra work. Now he *could* have earned about double his hourly rate if he chose to freelance his skills outside the company. But if he performed those same tasks on the job as extra work for AT&T, he would make 1.5 times his rate ... *plus* get company benefits ... *plus* get IRA contributions ... as well as other ancillary benefits that were well worth the effort. So, all told, freelancing wasn't a good idea for him.

So here's what my dad did instead: He worked on his real estate license and made *that* his side gig. Why? Because if he worked 10 hours per month and got one commission every three months, then 30 hours equated to a $6,000 commission. That's $200 per hour — ***more than four times*** what he got working for AT&T.

Here's something else to consider. There may very well be a side gig that consumes a ton of your time — say, four months — but then very little for the next four years.

Do these types of side gigs exist? Oh yeah, *lots* of them.

Remember my website Freelegalaid.com from earlier? That project required a lot of up-front time (although I did the work while I was being paid to sit at the computer lab and check IDs as part of a part-time job in law school).

Performing hundreds of hours for no pay certainly sucks. But when all that set-up work was completed, guess what?

It became a side gig that brought in $3,000 per month for just three hours of ongoing monthly work. That's ***$1,000 per hour***, more than double my attorney rate, and more than the average American worker gets paid each month for working full time. And not only that, but I continue to receive that income year after year.

Now THAT'S the power of a side gig! Are you beginning to see why we consider side gigs to be the foundation of the life you are looking for?

Reality check: For someone with fewer skills and no network, the side gig is likely to be something that requires more time per dollar. And that's fine. Start where you are. This might mean driving an Uber while you build your website side gig. It might mean doing deliveries while you build a coaching business. It might be mowing lawns while you build your network and figure out ways to leverage your skills to score a better gig.

You might even build a gig that takes a lot of your time so you can *sell* that gig. And when you do *that*, you'll have a chip at the table.

Moolah, my friend. Money is king. You can do a lot with cold hard cash, even buy a better side gig that throws off even *more* cash.

Of course, you could grow that one and sell it as well. Lather, rinse, repeat.

And hey, if you're rolling in cash, that's fine too. If your time has a high value, then you shouldn't blow your time building a website as your side gig. Instead, you should take that nice paycheck and use cash to buy a side gig that's doing well already.

Let's talk about some practical examples of side gigs that involve exchanging time for money. Selling your time is a fine start, and can be a great way to increase your monthly income while you develop a plan for something better.

Brian's Pool Cleaning

Brian is a maintenance supervisor. He has a good job. His income is stable, and he has insurance benefits. He's been a maintenance supervisor so long that he can do it with his eyes closed. Naturally, Brian is quite handy. He can fix anything, clean anything, probably do just about any mechanical task you throw his way. For the past five years Brian has cleaned the pools at a couple of apartment complexes every week. He makes $200 per month for each pool, which means he's got himself a nifty $400 monthly side gig.

All Brian has to do is head down to the apartments after work one day per week. He completes them both in an hour or so, and then heads home. Because the apartment complex pays for the supplies, he has no out-of-pocket expenses other than four miles worth of gas. Brian has no employees and he doesn't carry insurance. He even had the apartment complex owner sign off that Brian was not a licensed contractor and that he didn't carry insurance. This meant that if there was a liability problem such as someone tripping by the pool, the property owner's insurance would cover it and it wouldn't come back on Brian.

Sure, it would be awesome if Brian could make $400 per month and not have to work even one hour per week cleaning the pools. But $400 per month at one hour per week equates to $100 per hour. His pay at his day job is $22 per hour. His side gig is clearly far more lucrative than his day job.

Should Brian just start a full-time business cleaning pools? Maybe. It could be something that turns into a real business over time. But if Brian was to run a full-blown pool cleaning service, he wouldn't have a side gig. He'd have a business.

He'd have to charge more, work harder, and drive all over town every day. At the end of the month, he might make the same as he does with his regular job plus the $400 he's already making from his side gig. In other words, he may end up no better off. And he very likely could end up working more hours, taking more risk and not getting home on time for dinner every night.

Since he's just "the pool guy" in his side gig, and not an actual pool cleaning contractor carrying his own insurance, he doesn't need any liability insurance or bonding. He doesn't need any fancy accounting or corporate bookkeeping or tax filing. He still gets to write off his mileage, home office, and some of his business-related expenses. As his side gig currently stands, his $400 monthly income remains tax-free (because of his home office and mileage deductions) and makes a real difference in his life, not to mention his future retirement.

Ricardo's Hair Trim

I know several people who are trained to cut hair and have done it professionally for a living. Some were professional barbers or stylists who moved on to other careers. However, none lost their knack for giving a haircut, which of course gave them something valuable to sell as a side gig.

Ricardo cuts hair at home on the weekends or on his days off. He can take care of two people per week, adding a tidy $400 per month to his income. He can dictate when he is available, and chooses only the clients he wants. He doesn't have to dress nice or deal with salon politics. He can make as much extra money as he wants and use that skill every week, even though he may now be in a completely different career.

Even if Ricardo was still working at a salon, he could still do a haircut or dye job at home on a Saturday afternoon for 30 percent less than the salon. A professional may have to share a portion of their income with a salon or pay rent for their chair. Not so at home, where he eliminates those costs and is free to charge whatever he wants.

What other ways could *you* sell your time as a side gig?

I know people who spend a few hours a week managing some aspect of another person's life. They are personal assistants. They might run errands. They might get mail and make copies or scan things. They don't need any special skills, just honesty and a good work ethic. There are also *virtual* assistants. These people also help someone who is busy, but they don't have to run actual errands. They perform their duties virtually on the Internet. Example tasks might include accounting, social media management, digital graphics, copy editing, content creation, writing articles, or any number of various functions that entrepreneurs or small business people might need.

Ride sharing apps such as Uber and Lyft provide side gigs to those with a tidy car and a clean driving record. Piggyback lets you deliver packages using your own car as well. There are a number of platforms like these that allow people to easily find a side gig to generate extra income.

There are several online marketplaces that allow you to sell your time or talent from anywhere in the world. One such platform is called Upwork (formerly known as Odesk and Elance). You can list your availability as a virtual assistant or browse the listed opportunities and bid for the work. If you are a musician, you can sell your music to stock music sites. If you are a photographer, you can sell your photos on a number of different stock photo websites.

Bottom line: If you have a keyboard and an Internet connection, you can become part of a virtual team helping run a business — and get paid for it.

A word of warning, however. Side gigs that require your time can be dangerous because they can suck you into working more than you want or need. Find the right balance to make the most possible income for the least amount of time. This worked for Brian because he was efficient; both pools were near each other and could be done consecutively. For Ricardo, he can batch two or three haircuts into one block of time.

The "sell your time" side gig can easily become a real business. Now this might be fine for your particular situation; I am not here to tell you to keep it small. But if you really want to grow a side gig into a business, let me give you some cautions. I'll use my first business as an example.

I started Cricket Lawn Care when I was 19. I had a day job, and I was also a full-time student. Mowing lawns was just a side gig. A few lawns once a week produced as much money as my mall job made me in an entire month. The business was simple: one vehicle, one set of equipment, and no overhead. It was like Brian's pool cleaning service.

But I wanted the business to grow. I hated my mall job, which was selling ties and shirts at Nordstrom. I wanted to work entirely for myself. As I began to grow the business, I realized I needed to hire help. I also had to learn how to handle payroll and insurance. I had to borrow money from my aunt and uncle to buy more equipment. The business quickly grew from a little side gig into a real business. And if that's what you really want, you can do the same — just bear in mind that the growth from side gig to business has its costs. Be ready for them and understand that once you transition from non-business to business, it is now your day job. It will take all of your time. It will not produce "magic money" like a side gig. But make no mistake: It can still transform your life!

This book isn't about how to own and operate a business, it's about how to make side money from a non-business. However, I've owned a number of real businesses and they are absolutely worth the effort. There are many great books on the subject, including my book *Do What You Love!* And you can also join my tribe at DanaRobinson.com, where I do my best to help entrepreneurs and business owners as well as side-giggers.

Here are some other books you should consider reading before you jump into business as a new entrepreneur:

The E-Myth Revisited, by Michael Gerber

Good to Great, by Jim Collins

The Lean Startup, by Eric Ries

The 4-Hour Work Week, by Tim Ferriss

Rich Dad Poor Dad, by Robert Kiyosaki

How to Win Friends and Influence People, by Dale Carnegie

The Richest Man in Babylon, by George S. Clason

The $100 Startup, by Charles Guillebeau

Launch, by Jeff Walker

Zero to One, by Peter Thiel

ACTION STEPS

Self Assessment

- Ask yourself what can you do with your time that someone might pay you for? Make a list of anything you think you could do to sell your time. It does not have to be something highly skilled. My business partner Cory spent a year installing sprinklers in his neighborhood. He had no landscaping credentials, but had installed his own irrigation, and found that his neighbors needed the same.
- Here are some ideas to get you started:
    - Mow lawns
    - Cut hair
    - Clean pools
    - Wash windows
    - Detail cars
    - Run errands
    - Organize someone's life
    - Declutter a garage
    - Filing
    - Mailing

    - Teach a company something you do well (e.g. warehouse management, logistics, bookkeeping)
- Once you have your list, start asking around and figure out what people are charging to do these things, and then add that information to your list.

Chapter 15

Arbitrage

I'd like to tell you about a super cheap and easy way to build a side gig. In order to understand how to execute it, I need to first teach you about a fairly complex economic principle. I'm going to teach you about *arbitrage*.

Let's start with the Wikipedia definition:

In economics and finance, arbitrage ... is the practice of taking advantage of a price difference between two or more markets: striking a combination of matching deals that capitalize upon the imbalance, the profit being the difference between the market prices.

In the world of big money, arbitrageurs look for a small difference between a stock or commodity price in one market, and then exploit that difference. For example, if the price of gold is $1,501 in the U.S., and after considering the currency exchange, the same gold is $1,500 in Japan, an arbitrageur will buy as much gold in the Japan market as possible for $1,500 and sell it immediately in the U.S. market for $1,501. That $1.00 difference might seem small. But when the expert investor moves a million ounces (on paper), that can add up to $1 million in profit just by finding a slight difference in price gap between two markets.

Every day, savvy experts spend hours scouring the markets for arbitrage opportunities. These generally don't last long. Why? Because the window closes quickly once arbitrageurs exploit the price gap. For example, in the scenario above, as arbitrageurs see and pounce on the small price gap, the price in Japan would slowly rise toward $1,501, and the gap eventually closes. Fortune rewards the quick for those willing to seize the moment before others.

Arbitrage can become more complicated when it comes to sophisticated financial instruments such as derivatives — in which tradable instruments are constructed of "call" and/or "put" options — and debt obligations, commodities, and stock. If you can arbitrage the markets, then good for you! I can't. It's out of my league. If it's out of your league, too, then I have a much better way to employ arbitrage that anyone can do.

Let me give you a concrete example of a regular guy doing arbitrage to make money on the side.

Gary's Video Games

I had a resourceful law clerk working for me recently. Gary was bootstrapping his way through law school, working for the law school in addition to my clerking duties. He had a side gig as well. It was a little something he called, "Craigslist arbitrage."

What is Craigslist arbitrage? It means buying something on Craigslist for one price and then selling the same item immediately on eBay for a higher price. Gary was exploiting a price difference between Craigslist (less expensive) and eBay (more expensive).

Why is there a discrepancy in price between these two large marketplaces? Because Craigslist requires buyers to coordinate with each other and make physical contact for delivery. In this way, Craigslist lacks efficiency because buyers and sellers can't safely facilitate a sale without meeting in person. In addition, Craigslist is regionalized locally while eBay is a worldwide market of willing buyers and sellers. eBay has near perfect efficiency and global reach.

To arbitrage Craigslist and eBay, you need to buy something on Craigslist for one price, and then sell it on eBay for a higher price. Pretty simple, right? That's the beauty of arbitrage. However, simple doesn't always mean easy. Here's the problem: You have to spend a lot of time trying to find the right products at the right price. If done badly, this is a terrible side gig. You don't want to spend dozens of hours per month hunting for deals and then even more time selling those items at a higher price.

Gary avoided this inefficiency by using RSS feed to monitor new listings on Craigslist. And he only bought items he knew a lot about — video games. He knew how to buy them, what questions to ask, and he also knew how much he could sell them for on eBay. This allowed him to use simple technology to snap up the good deals and then run around town picking up his treasures when he had the time. He would then double his price on every eBay sale. He made a hefty monthly sum to supplement his student income, and he didn't have to work hard to do it.

Why wouldn't the people selling video games on Craigslist just sell them on eBay and make double their money? Laziness! Ambivalence! Busyness! All of which become synonyms for "opportunity."

Sellers gravitate immediately to Craigslist for several reasons. For starters, people don't want to hassle with eBay. They don't want to set up an account, configure the various settings on their auction, deal with buyer questions, handle shipping, etc. For many, it just isn't worth the extra money. They'd rather go to Craigslist and wait for the buyer to show up and hand them cold, hard cash.

This presents an arbitrage opportunity for those willing to do a little work on the Craigslist side to procure the goods, and then handle the eBay work on the selling side. The reward is a very nice little non-business that can make money indefinitely. The key is to specialize like Gary. Find something you can become expert at, and get to know the values for those products on eBay. You can also add to your income by finding those same products at swap meets, flea markets, and garage sales.

The Book Liquidator

One of my relatives is famous for having side gigs. Uncle Herman always had a day job. In fact, he took a full retirement from that job recently. However, throughout his career he always had a side hustle. One of the best was his little book liquidation business. It isn't too different from Gary's arbitrage above.

As ebooks became more widespread, the value of paper books began to tumble. It is still tumbling. But when it first started to trend downward, one thing happened pretty fast: Small used bookstores started to fail. The result of so many used bookstores failing was that there were a lot of used books available in large quantities. What Uncle Herman did was genius.

Herman bought the entire inventory of a used bookstore. He had the garage space to store them. His purchase was on the order of a few thousand dollars for thousands of books. He cataloged them into software that managed his inventory and then connected that inventory software to several online used book sites, including Amazon. Because he bought in bulk, his average cost for a book was ten cents. He could sell a book from anywhere from $1 to $10. He also made a couple of dollars in shipping and handling. He had a little workshop set up in his garage so he could easily wrap the books in shipping paper, print a label from his software, and in just one hour ship all of the sales for that day. His return per book was never less than 10 times what he paid. When shipping and handling was added, his profitability was more like 30 times his investment. Uncle Herman's side gig went on for many years. It required little work, was not stressful, and he didn't need much up-front or ongoing capital. It took him an hour a day to run, but that small time investment resulted in thousands of profit per month. Who would have thought that a dying marketplace for paper books could breathe life into a side gig that generated thousands of dollars per month … for years?

The Last Chance!

Unless you've been trapped in my uncle's used book garage for decades, you already know about Nordstrom, the high-end retail chain. You've also probably heard about their infamous return policy. They'll pretty much take anything back. Some people abuse this policy (more on that in a minute), but most return items for legitimate reasons. For example, if you buy some penny loafers at Nordstrom, wear them for a few days and get blisters, you can return them. Now you can see why their prices might be a little higher: They need to build that loss into the purchase price. They have to protect their margins to be sure you can return something they won't be able to sell as new.

What do they do with all those returns? They certainly don't put them back on the shelf. This is Nordstrom, remember, the iconic, high-class joint. What they do instead is ship those returns to a special store for liquidation. It's called Nordstrom Last Chance Clearance Store and it's located in the basement of a funky mall in Arizona. Yes, there really is a store in the Southwest where all those mildly worn shoes and clothes get a second life by being sold at steep discounts.

I love the store because I can get a pair of Ferragamo shoes for $49 rather than $599. Have they been worn? Yes, maybe once, maybe for a week. Either way, those shoes love my feet and they are otherwise too expensive for me to justify spending the full retail price. So I shop for shoes, suits, and even expensive jeans at Last Chance. But this little basement retail store is not without a few hazards. I'm not talking about scarce parking or treacherous footing. I'm talking about the other shoppers. You know those "Black Friday" mobs the day after Thanksgiving in which frenzied shoppers will practically maul each other for the best deals? Well, fights like that are real at The Last Chance. Very real.

There's a reason shoppers might get aggressive. How about a $1,500 handbag for $100 to $300? Or $300 denim jeans for under $70? You can imagine why people want to grab what's fresh on the rack as fast as they can. The store does a great job at managing the crazy shoppers. It can make for some fun people-watching.

I discovered that there is a small group of people who don't shop for themselves at Last Chance. They shop for resale. These people buy things they know they can turn around and sell on eBay, Craigslist or, in some cases, their own websites. They are very much like Gary and his video games. They are engaging in discount retail arbitrage. They can buy Ferragamo shoes for $49 and sell them for $150. The buyer who gets them at $150 is still happy to not pay $599 retail, and the arbitrageur makes three times her investment.

Remember Gary who bought video games on Craigslist and sold them for a healthy profit on eBay? He succeeded because he specialized in something he knew well. The same is true for anyone who wants to play the arbitrage game with jeans, shoes or handbags. You must know your market very well so that you can quickly determine how much you should pay for product. Can you sell your item if it's slightly damaged? Maybe. And you can only know that sort of thing if you know your market inside and out.

Whether you are going to arbitrage using Craigslist, Nordstrom Last Chance, garage sales or thrift stores, only deal in items you know well. Focus on just a few things. This ensures that your little side gig makes you money consistently and without risk.

Outsource Your Creativity & Insource the Work

Let's say you don't want to run around buying video games or go hunting in the basement of a mall in Arizona to find your arbitrage opportunity. Could you arbitrage something virtual? Absolutely. Let me explain.

You can offer a service in the U.S. that you don't actually fulfill yourself. How? By outsourcing the task to a person or company in another country that can do the work for a significantly lower fee than you would charge. Here's how that works: Let's say you want to offer a service of creating company logos. You offer this to your U.S. customers through a website that you own and control, and then when you get orders you simply outsource the actual artwork to a small company in India, Pakistan, Indonesia or Philippines. Because of the difference in national economies around the globe, logo designers in other countries can charge much less and you can pocket the difference as the middle man.

What might this look like as a side gig? Let's return to our example of company logos. In this case, you could offer a service that creates logos for companies in the U.S. You could offer a flat fee of, say, $100 to create three sample logos. But wait — you don't know how to create logos! No problem, you aren't going to create them. Instead, you are going to outsource this to someone who does. And you are going to pay them $35 for this, and keep the $65 difference for yourself.

Why would someone hire you for $100 if they can hire an offshore firm themselves for $35? Because you speak good English. Because you understand Western business. Because you can take a phone call during business hours in United States time zones. (Because you can take a phone call, *period!*) People will hire you and feel secure in working with someone who understands American-style branding. Your job becomes one of marketing yourself on the one hand, and then clearly communicating with your outsourced graphic team on the other.

Where do you find the graphic artist who will do your logos for $35? Upwork.com is one source. Another is Fiverr.com. These are just two of many sources for overseas contractors who can become part of your side gig, and allow you to outsource...*you*!

What you are doing is arbitraging the differences in labor prices between a foreign country and your own country. You are outsourcing yourself. You are arbitraging yourself. Whatever skill you have that's marketable, there's surely someone in the world you can pay to do it for you at a lower fee.

ACTION STEPS

Arbitrage Experiment

I'm going to ask you to try a couple of arbitrage experiments. You'll need to have an eBay account to do this.

- First, pick something you know well enough to understand its inherent value. It may not be video games. Maybe it's Beanie Babies, Pokemon Cards, or Lladro figurines. It might be DVDs or CDs. It might be branded denim. You are then going to start watching those items on eBay and learn their final sales prices. After three to four weeks of doing this, buy several items in that category from sellers on Craigslist, or from local markets such as thrift shops, swap meets or estate sales.

- Next, list them on eBay and set your reserve price below the price you have seen the other products sell for in your research.
- When your auction ends, congratulate yourself on what may be your first arbitrage win. Use your profit to buy more things and keep it going. Or, you may just do this exercise for the purpose of understanding a very important aspect of business: You bought low and sold high. You made a profit. This is the very thing you are going to do with your side gig. It is the core to all business transactions. Thus, even if you don't plan to make Craigslist arbitrage your side gig, I'd like you to do this exercise so that you get the emotional connection that comes from having done it.

Chapter 16

Real Estate

Real estate deserves a book of its own. But I want to talk briefly about how to make real estate a side gig because, trust me, there are many ways to make real estate a business. It has been a big part of my business life. For a period of time I was fully invested in real estate with nearly 100 units, and it was far more than a side gig. But I have a couple of stories about real estate as a non-business that are worth talking about.

Hippie Vagabond Mr. T

I have this cool friend I can only describe as a hippie vagabond. I don't mean it in a bad way. But when a guy has beads braided into his beard, and he wears more jewelry than Mr. T, what else can I say? He's like a hippie Mr. T who vagabonds the world. In fact, the first time I met him I asked where he was from.

"I'm a citizen of the world," he said. He attends music festivals around the globe. He posts Facebook photos from remote islands in places you've never heard of. He may be praying in Tibet one week and be partying in Ibiza the next.

What did my hippie friend do to enable him to become a vagabonding festival rat? He purchased two properties in the 1990s. Not huge investments. In fact, they were quite modest. Hippie Mr. T reached a point in his professional life where he needed a long break. So he quit his job, sold most of what he owned, and decided to vagabond until he ran out of money. But he kept those two little house rentals, hiring a bookkeeper to receive the income and deal with the property manager on his behalf. After covering the mortgage and expenses, he pocketed a few hundred dollars per month from each of those two houses. Being the hippie vagabond, all he had to do in the beginning was to do what came naturally: namely, travel and live simply, existing on the small excess income he had from those properties.

Hippie Mr. T originally hoped to make his little excursion last a year. When I met him, he had been in vagabond mode for *eight years*. He hadn't needed to work because he had that tiny little income from those two rental properties. Not only were those two houses financing his perpetual retirement, but he was also paying down the mortgages, slowly increasing his wealth. At the same time, over those eight years rents were rising. Which meant his income was increasing, his asset base was growing, and all the while he was free to do whatever he wanted, wherever he wanted.

Over the years, he got a little bored. He discovered that he had an eye for jewelry of a certain style. You know, that organic hippie style. So he's spent the past few years buying jewelry from markets in India, Thailand and other exotic destinations, and then selling it in other markets, such as the U.S., Israel and Latin America. That gives him even greater financial freedom, and an excuse to travel to places he enjoys to have tea with his vendors, or attend an electronic dance music festival where he might also be shopping for unique stones, gems, or hemp bracelets.

Real estate can become a side gig. But in order to make real estate a side gig, you have to obtain real estate that doesn't require much of your time, and also has a predictable flow of income. From personal experience, I can tell you that 90 units of apartments is *not* a side gig. However, two houses can be. A fourplex might be perfect. Even one house or condo can generate a few hundred dollars per month in excess income.

What else can you do with real estate to create a side gig? How about the "Fonzie Flat"? I'm dating myself a bit here, but in the television sitcom "Happy Days," the cool dude Fonzarelli (aka "Fonzie" or "The Fonz") lived in a flat above the Cunningham's house. If you own your house, you can create a room in your attic, basement or above your garage with a separate entrance and rent it out. You can make your side gig owning and renting your Fonzie Flat and generate hundreds of dollars per month without any significant investment or much ongoing effort.

A Fonzie Flat can also be something you rent short term through websites such as AirBnB, Love Home Swap, OneFineStay, or VRBO. These websites allow you to rent out your room or an apartment for a day or two, or maybe a week at a time. I have personally done this and have had substantial success renting short term. The income is far greater than renting by the month. It also means you now have a nifty little unit for your out-of-town friends and family to use when you don't have French vacation renters staying in your Fonzie Flat. You don't even need a full Fonzie Flat to make side gig money on your house. You can do the same by renting a single room in your house. AirBnB even lets you rent your sofa to a traveling couch surfer. Or consider moving out for the weekend and make big bucks by renting your entire house for a few days. I had a friend who lived in an urban loft who would rent his entire apartment on AirBnB and then go stay at a friend's house for a night or two whenever it was rented. He would share a slice of the income with his buddy and still pocket nearly enough to pay his entire mortgage for the month.

You might consider an empty lot that you currently own, or part of your home or office. Could you possibly rent some of that space? Could you sublet your garage? Make your real estate work for you. Whether you become another hippie vagabond Mr. T, or just generate $400 per month in extra income, look at creative ways to make your real estate a side gig.

Brokering, Wholesaling & Flips

Obtaining a real estate license can provide multiple pathways to side gig income. Brokers save money on commissions on their own deals. Brokers can let agents hang their license for a fee. Brokers can be part of a team that does fix-and-flip deals. Brokers can wholesale properties. Of course, you can help people buy or sell real estate for a commission, and that can add up fast.

You can do many of the same things with a real estate agent license, rather than a broker's license. But you might consider having an agent's license for a few years and then leveling up to the broker's license later.

Whether or not you are licensed, you can also do something pretty cool called "wholesaling." Wholesaling is where you find a property that you believe is undervalued and you make an offer to buy it. But you list the buyer as yourself, "or assignee", so that you can take the contract to an investor and sell them your position. Most wholesalers make $5,000 per deal or more. They have almost no risk because they build a contingency into the agreement that gives them two to three weeks to withdraw from the deal without any consequences. During that time, they find a buyer, take a cut and move on to the next deal.

Sometimes the wholesales lead to flips. Meaning, the wholesaler will work out a deal with the buyer to "get the re-list" on the house and then they'll use their salesperson's license to sell it. This means once the buyer/flipper has bought the house and has fixed it up and wants to sell it, you'll be the listing agent/brokerage.

Managing Property

I've already described how I managed an apartment complex when I was in law school. That's a real estate play. I didn't need a license to do it. But when it comes to managing other people's property, you can get a license pretty easily and then start managing a few properties. It's an easy side gig that can generate monthly cash flow that requires little time.

Aysen is a great example. She was always helping the owner of the small apartment complex where she lived. Eventually, the owner asked her to help fill the units with foreign students.

Aysen was from Germany and found that she could market the units to German exchange students coming to the U.S. She was paid based on her success, and didn't have to work hard. She still had a day job, but made real side money by helping her landlord make more money.

AirBnB and VRBO

There's a big opportunity to find a property in the short term rental market (STR, as they now call it). Basically, you look for a property that may only fetch $1,000 per month in traditional rent, and see if you can short term rent it for more. If you can, then when you buy the property you are going to make more than the previous owner, and thus you are paying less than the property is worth.

You don't actually have to buy the property either. You can rent a property from a landlord who is friendly to STR, and then *you* short term rent it. You collect the difference between the base rent you pay and the higher rent you generate from renting it on AirBnB or VRBO.

Another way to play the STR game is to offer to manage other properties for absentee owners who pay you a commission on the rental income. In many states, you don't need to be licensed to broker real estate on rentals of less than 30 days.

Some people build a side gig property management business just doing STRs.

ACTION STEPS

Brainstorming

- Assess your real estate situation. Do you own your home? Does it have the space to create a Fonzie flat? Some homes have a room that would only need two things: a new exterior door and a way to lock out the interior from access to the house. That's how many homeowners create a cheap Fonzie Flat. Or what about your attic?

Research

- Look on VRBO.com and AirBnB.com to see if homes in your area are available and compare the available rentals with your own house.

Assess Your Market

- Do you have some cash that you could use to buy a house or small complex? Talk to a local realtor about getting a 2-4 unit complex with as little as 3.5% down with FHA financing. Do the math: Can you buy a complex and have it pay for the costs? If so, then when rents rise in the coming years, you'll begin to have cash flow, a nifty side gig that doesn't take much effort and pays for itself over time.

Chapter 17

Loans and Loaning Your Credit

There's an old book by George Clason titled, *The Richest Man in Babylon.* It's the story of a fictional character from Biblical days who learns the lesson of managing his assets. He becomes a lender, rather than a borrower, and leverages his assets to grow his wealth.

I don't want to make this chapter an extensive treatment on lending, but I want to point out a few unique approaches to deploying credit in ways that can generate real revenue, and can even substitute as a side gig.

The first thing you could consider is making loans with the cash you have. You can do this casually, over a handshake, but that carries great risk. It's far better to have an attorney draw up a promissory note, and then get some form of security. That might be as simple as acting like a pawn shop and holding valuable property until the loan is paid. Or it might be as sophisticated as securing a loan against real property in the form of a trust deed.

A trust deed (or similar instrument depending on the state) allows you to foreclose on real estate when someone doesn't pay you. You can also use what's called a UCC filing to secure against general assets of an individual or a business. Banks require that when they loan to people and businesses.

Making loans can generate significant income if you are willing to take the risk. That's because the only people who will borrow from you are not able to borrow from a traditional bank, or they wouldn't be asking you for a loan. Depending on state limitations on interest, you might fetch 15% to 20% annual interest. This means deploying $100,000 that you may have in your nest egg or in a 401k that could make you as much as $20,000 per year by doing private lending.

Now consider what I just said above. If you draw from your own sources of income, borrowing from yourself at almost no interest, you'd be borrowing at a very low rate and then loaning at a high rate. That's an arbitrage opportunity that may give you serious income without actually having to come up with the cash out of your own pocket.

Many lenders look for ways to specialize so that they can avoid risks and invest where they best know the market and opportunities. For example, some people I know only loan as a first or second loan against real estate. Others only loan for short term on fix-and-flip deals. Others only loan on business assets with a UCC against the entire business.

If you get into this activity, be sure you do your research, learn the industry and then use good legal advice to protect yourself.

I know of one investor who loaned $400,000 to a business. The lender didn't file any security documents. When the business went into bankruptcy, the investor lost everything. Be careful.

Factoring

"Factoring" is similar to lending, but commands higher premiums and tends to be more secure than lending. Factoring (a strange word, I know) means that you actually buy someone's accounts receivable. You buy what someone owes a business, rather than loaning to the business.

For example, Suzy makes expensive blankets that she sells to retail stores around the country. When Suzy ships blankets to a store, the store owes Suzy money that they won't pay for 60 days. Meanwhile, Suzy needs money. Suzy goes to Dana's Factors (not a real business, although I did once own a factoring business). Suzy sells Dana's Factors $10,000 in open receivables. Dana's Factors pays Suzy $6,000 of that up front and then Suzy assigns all rights to the AR to Dana's Factors. Dana's Factors notifies the accounts to direct payments to Dana and not to Suzy. Then, when the account pays Dana, Dana turns around and pays Suzy the remainder, minus fees of about 2% to 3% per month. That means Dana's Factors makes between 24% to 36% per year on the money advanced. And the AR is owned by Dana, not Suzy, so there's greater security than loaning Suzy money directly.

If you want to get into factoring, join the Factoring Association and start learning the ropes. It's an interesting business that can be run as a side gig and generate substantial cash flow on either your own money, or on money you borrow at a lower rate.

Credit Card Points

Let me share a unique twist on using credit to make money as a side gig. My partner Nate had an Amazon Visa with a high limit. He would allow one of his business partners to use the credit card for inventory. The business partner might run up a $50,000-per-month bill and pay it off each month. That meant no one was paying interest. What did Nate get for loaning his right to use his credit card? He got Amazon gift certificates that added up to tens of thousands of dollars. Nate could spend that on anything he wanted on Amazon, so it was the same as cash to him, and it cost him nothing.

You can do the same with letting a colleague use your airline points card so that you get the points and they get to use your open credit. You could even charge a fee for the service.

True story: There are people making more than $1,000 per month doing this. As long as you feel secure about the person using your card, the pay is solid and there's no time required on your part.

Chapter 18

The Home Run, the Holy Grail, the Big Win

You may have asked yourself while reading this book whether you can take the idea of a side gig and do something really, really big. Can you make hundreds of thousands per year in a side gig? Can you make millions?

The answer is … yes, actually. Let me tell you about a couple home run side gigs.

Aviation Company

Cliff is a pilot who owns a small air charter company. But he doesn't fly for a living. It turns out that hiring pilots is pretty cheap. So Cliff doesn't need to fly as a pilot for a living, even though he can fly if he wants to. For years he matched people who wanted to take a trip with an aircraft and pilot. In the beginning, he was merely a matchmaker. He just had to build a client list of people who trusted him to find a great charter at a fair price.

Cliff slowly built a business that catered to high-end clients.

He didn't even need to own his own plane. Aircraft are often owned by wealthy people who do not use them full-time. Instead, the wealthy person might own the plane and use it once or twice a month and allow third parties to charter the plane for a fee. The person with the aircraft might let someone like Cliff rent the plane for $2,000 per hour, or maybe even less. Cliff could then charge his full price to his customers, and make a profit on the difference.

Cliff built his charter business until he had multiple aircraft active at one time. The money he made was quite substantial. Within a few years, Cliff bought a very expensive plane himself, paying cash. He then found several contract-based pilots who were available at any time to fly for Cliff's customers. Soon Cliff was making three times what he was before, and a couple of years later, he bought another plane. With two aircraft of his own, and a list of third-party planes he could subcontract, he had a flourishing business. "But wait!" you might say, echoing what I've repeatedly told you throughout this book. "That's a real business, not a side gig!"

Well, let's look at the reality: Cliff works from home. He has no employees. He has low overhead. He outsources the booking to an independent contractor. He no longer has to do any marketing. His customers keep coming back and refer others. What he does now is hardly a job. He might work an hour or two in a day. He can take off weeks, even months, to travel. He built his business to function as a non-business. And he's made millions of dollars.

The aircraft he owns are worth millions. He has seven figures coming in each year. (He has put that money to work for him as well.) Cliff has hit the ultimate side gig home run, and he's under 40 years old.

He's not alone. While the following example is not one of my personal friends, I know a second person who has done almost exactly the same thing in the same industry. These two demonstrate the real possibility of creating a non-business that we might call the Holy Grail of entrepreneurship: making millions per year without the "normal" business responsibilities.

Examine.com

Sol Orwell is 32 years old and makes more than $1 million per year without any employees. No offices, no inventory.

His business, Examine.com, focuses on fitness, nutrition and supplements.

I don't know Sol personally, but he's certainly hit a home run with his business, and not in the way that so many entrepreneurs dream of doing. Most entrepreneurs dream of creating a startup, hiring staff, and getting an office. Hiring even more staff. And then when they have 100 employees and $30 million in annual revenue, they'll sell their venture and sail off into the sunset. This is not how Sol sees things.

Sol has built a non-business; his million dollar company is a side gig! He's making over a million dollars per year with no employees and no office. How does he do it? He outsources and subcontracts. He's even managed to share the equity in his venture with people who help run things while never needing to hire anyone or create a "normal" business environment. He doesn't need a human resources director. He doesn't need to do tax filings or employment law compliance. He never has to stress about how to make payroll because he *has no payroll.* And he's never short on cash either.

According to Forbes, there were 30,174 "nonemployer" companies that made between $1 million to $2.5 million in 2013. That's a lot of companies in which the only staff is the owner. How many of those are what we would consider *non-businesses*? Well, even though companies with that level of revenue commonly have staff — a typical company with $2 million in revenue will have a dozen employees — it *is* possible to maintain these businesses as side gigs if the owner removes herself as much as possible from the daily operations. This can be understandably difficult, but it *can* be done if the owner works themselves "out of the job" starting on day one. In other words, you must start the business as a non-business, and even when you *do* get offices and staff, you must not be necessary, so to speak. One step in this direction, for example, is to not include an office for yourself when leasing your space.

Sounds almost impossible, right? Well, that just speaks to the difficulty I've described often in these pages: namely, that reaping side gig benefits when playing in the big boy arena of "real" business can be a challenge.

Sol managed to do it because he built the business that way on purpose, avoiding hiring employees or renting office space. If you want or need those things, then you'll have to be extremely diligent about maintaining the low-involvement and low-stress hallmarks that make the side gig such an attractive alternative to running a "real" business.

I'm going to let you in on one more of my own secrets. I've spent the past decade building a fairly successful law practice. I'm a founding partner of Techlaw LLP, which has more than a dozen attorneys associated with it. My own practice group has two full time attorneys, a paralegal and me.

When I decided to take a sabbatical and spend a year in Bali, I also decided to experiment with my own theories about running side gigs. I experimented with my law practice. The question was whether I could live abroad and work less than an hour a day while still making the same amount of money.

I worked for six months to create the model for a law practice so that it functioned without me being the bottleneck. I then took off for Bali. I'm here now, writing this book. Since I have been in Bali I've drafted two other books, and have written a first draft of a law school casebook (800 pages of legal stuff that would bore most of you to tears). I've definitely succeeded in making the time to do what I wanted to do: write, surf, catch up on sleep, and travel. In the past year, I've been around Indonesia, Spain, France, Holland, Singapore, Australia and even ended up in Arkansas for the first time in my life.

Did it work financially? Was I successful at making my law practice a side gig? Well, I worked less than 10 hours per week, and most weeks about five hours was dedicated to my practice. That worked. What about the income? Well, my income *increased!* It turns out that sometimes your best side gig is the business you are doing full-time. Before coming to Bali I was overworked and overwhelmed. By empowering my team and removing myself from the day-to-day, I ended up providing better service to my clients, better mentorship to my team, and as a result my practice grew and flourished.

ACTION STEPS

Vision Board Time!

- I'd like you to create a vision board. This requires magazines, photos, paste and some cardboard. Take half of a day some weekend when you have the mental space to dream. Start by going through photos (print them if you are finding photos online). Cut out photos and words from magazines and paste all of this onto a poster board of any size (make it as big as you'd like). Once you're done, place this in your house, room or apartment where you can see it for a week or two. Then put it away in a closet. You'll go back to it in a year or two. For now, the vision board exercise is a way to free your mind of restraints and tap into your deeper desires.

Sometimes starting a side gig can feel small. Maybe you'll never make it big. But don't sell yourself short — your side gig could very well become a million dollar business. It also might just be a stepping stone to the next thing, and *that* might be the home run. Remind yourself periodically that you have bigger things ahead. Never forget that your side gig is part of a plan to break yourself free financially. Don't get dragged down by thinking that your little side gig will "only" be a

$400 per month thing. The side gig is a step, and as you take that step, don't forget to keep your eye on the bigger prize. You'll get there.

Chapter 19

Show Me the Money!

When it comes down to the freedom that the Opt Out Life can give you, *money* is what it comes down to. Not that money is all that matters. Definitely not. But it *is* a tool you need so that you can get the life you want. That's because it buys you something most valuable of all: time.

Control over your time is the goal. To get there, we need money.

So let's talk about money and how it relates to creating your first side gig.

Good news: Getting into a side gig can be cheap and easy. But if you DO have some of the green stuff, don't be afraid to leverage its power.

I knew a woman who used some of her career earnings to buy a couple of coupon websites for $30,000. Now, $30K might seem like a lot of money to most people, but if you DO have that sort of reserve available, you could consider the opportunity of, say, purchasing a website that already is earning $2K per month. Which means you would make your money back in a little over a year. And of course if you improve the site, you'll make your money back even sooner.

Choosing a side gig is relative to your cash. I have worked that calculus into this book because people with $30K want to opt out as much as people with $300. If you have between $300 and $3,000 on hand, then starting from scratch is probably your best option.

If you have more than $3K, then you might be better off finding a side gig that is already operational, and then buying it. That's a way to use your cash to skip the up-front work that is required to start from scratch.

Money may also be a way to acquire a side gig that is less correlated to your time. For example, if you don't have the money to buy a side gig *and* you also happen to have a short list of skills, well, then your first side gig may be something that requires you to sell your time (consulting, driving, delivering, etc.).

Another option is to start a side gig around those skills that will earn you passive income. Side gigs in this category include creating e-learning courses, web publishing, and software.

Conversely, if you have money but not much in the way of skills, then you can use your money to acquire a side gig that someone else has built, and then learn how to grow it and keep the money flowing.

If you're fortunate to have both skills *and* money, well, then congrats — you'll have the choice of either building something with your own skills, or buying something and leveraging your skills to make that particular side gig better.

To summarize, here's how to evaluate your money matrix:

- **No Money/No Skills**: Start with selling your time
- **Money/No Skills**: Buy something and learn all you can to make it better
- **No Money/Skills**: Build something around your skills from scratch
- **Money/Skills**: Choose to build or buy, leverage skills either way

For instance, if your list includes "drive an Uber" as a side gig, but you do indeed have skills or money, then cross off Uber on your list of potential side gigs for the reasons we've already discussed.

However, if you don't have skills or money, and Uber *isn't* on your list, then it's time to add that one, plus other similar platforms, such as TaskRabbit, GrubHub, DoorDash, Amazon Flex and the many others that have been created.

And don't forget that you're not just looking at this as a short-term opportunity. Your side gig can literally be *an asset you can sell* in the future.

Here are a few places to perform your own due diligence:

Flippa

Appbusinessbrokers.com

Sunbrokers

BizQuest

BizBuySell

Businessforsale.com

Loopnet (for physical businesses)

eBay

Craigslist

The MLS (ask a broker or agent for help)

This is a good exercise for all future side giggers because even if you can't buy a side gig right now, you might SELL yours once you've built it from scratch. Also, it's helpful to see how much people are selling various side gigs and businesses for so that you have a better sense of the ultimate value of what you intend to build.

If you are using my Side Gig Calculator, there are two sheets to focus on here:

(1) Your money: A sheet with an easy-to-use tool that lets you score your gigs based on how much money it will cost to acquire or launch. This will ensure that you don't break the bank on creating your side gig.

(2) Future side gig sale: A sheet to calculate how much your gig is going to be worth some day. Again, this is speculative but worth considering. This sheet shows several examples in various categories.

Chapter 20

Why Sunday Night Sucks (But Doesn't Have To)

I can remember a few times in my life when Sunday night sucked.

Why did it suck? Because Monday was coming ... which meant the bliss of the weekend was over.

Now, during a few phases of life, that Monday thing was a J-O-B. A job I didn't want to go to. A week of stress and long days. Another week of Groundhog Day.

And look, even when I was self-employed I *still* was not exempt from the "Sunday Night Feeling."

Why? Because I was a victim of my own success. And because I was being pulled in eight different directions (It felt like more than that, but hey, octopus is my spirit animal, and I only have eight tentacles.)

So let me ask you: Does Sunday night suck for *you*?

If the answer is yes, then you need a side gig. A side gig is part of what saves you from the Sunday night sinkhole of despair.

Let me talk about what's at the core of all of this angst. It's *stress*. The big American killer.

Now, stress is not completely avoidable, and in some cases it can be somewhat justified. For instance, "real" businesses cause stress. And that’s understandable because businesses have so much more at stake.

But our little ol' side gigs? They should not cause you stress. You learned that early on in this book.

So what causes stress? Well, when it comes to business, most stress comes from *risk*. When there’s risk, you lose sleep. When there’s risk, you have to hustle. When there’s risk, you are always looking over your shoulder.

Sure, some stress comes from simply being busy. Busy stress is something you can control when you understand the value of your time. But, what about the stress that comes from risk? Too many people ignore this until they're already too deep in a business or side gig to do anything about it. So how do we reduce risk?

We pick a side gig that isn’t risky!

Seriously, you'd be surprised how easily this is overlooked. I have a few unique metrics to measure risk. Here are a few things that will help you evaluate how risky — and thus stressful — your side gig will be:

- How much does liability insurance cost?
- What are the consequences of sloppy work?
- Is litigation common?
- Is a professional license required?

- What are the consequences to blowing everything off for a few weeks?
- Can you be sick for a few days and not think about the side gig at all?

How do you answer these questions? You'll have to ask around. Let's take these one at a time.

How much does liability insurance cost?

Ask an insurance agent. (You'll need to consider buying liability insurance once your side gig is up and running anyhow.)

What are the consequences of sloppy work?

Ask others in the industry. Go to a meetup and start asking questions of people who are already doing this type of gig.

Is litigation common?

Ask an attorney. (You'll need to get to know good business and IP attorneys as your venture grows anyhow.)

Is a professional license required?

Um ... Google it. It's typically obvious for areas such as real estate, law, banking, beauty, financial, etc.

What are the consequences to blowing everything off for a few weeks?

Really think through what you're doing and how your gig will make money. And then apply some logic as you evaluate this question.

Can you be sick for a few days and not think about the side gig at all?

This is another great question to ask at a meetup or networking event.

You should be getting the idea here. You want a side gig that is relatively stress-free.

Of course, very few gigs are completely free of risk. So the goal becomes finding the ones with the *least* risk, and then scoring those high on your worksheet.

Bottom line: Seriously consider the whole risk/stress angle from the very beginning as you build your side gig venture.

Chapter 21

Doing What You Like (Doing What You Love ... Revisited)

I'd like to give you some much-needed nuance on one of the most critical aspects of your side gig.

More specifically, I'm revisiting what I like to call the "do what you love" factor.

Yep, that ever-popular notion that I famously shot down…the one you *didn't* want to hear. The one that meant crossing off ideas on your list that were so warm and fuzzy.

Yeaaaaah, sorry about that. But good news: We're coming back to that ... with a reprieve of sorts!

In case you forgot, or don't know what I'm talking about here, the basic idea of my previous advice was this:

Forget about doing what you love. Instead, focus on something you're good at.

Now, I'm not taking that advice back, not one bit. But look, I'm not a total Scrooge. You don't have to hate what you're doing. I do want you to at least *like* what you're doing.

That's because you won't succeed at doing something you hate. You have to feel at least pretty good about what you are doing with your time. And that means doing something you find likable.

For example, if you're the type who prefers to sit in the quiet and write rather than networking and socializing, then you shouldn’t pick a side gig that requires regular social outings where you're chatting up prospects and making new acquaintances.

And conversely, if meeting new people is your thing and the idea of sitting at home writing articles feels like a small prison sentence, well, then ditch the side gig ideas that would chain you to a laptop.

I believe this is so crucial that I’ve created a separate column in my Side Gig Calculator to score it as an important factor that you should weigh.

Here’s the thing: It’s not about whether you like *the subject.* It’s about *liking the work itself.* In other words, you have to be okay with the tasks required, not necessarily the thing itself.

For example, you might love travel and think that doing something related to travel will qualify as likable. But if the actual *work* for that particular side gig means answering customer service emails for a travel site you've created, then put aside your travel bug and ask yourself this: "Do I enjoy dealing with people and solving their problems?"

For those who are using my Side Gig Calculator, if your answer is "yes" — *and* if you also like travel, then you’ll score that gig as a 5. However, if you like travel but hate people, well, then you'd score it a 1. Got it?

Now, let's look for a side gig that leverages what you already know how to do. This is important because it can take years to gain some skills, and we're going to assume you'd rather not invest, say, 8,000 hours of your time if you want a side gig *now*, am I right?

So here's a little secret that many people don't realize: ***Doing what you are good at is often doing something you LIKE.***

Ha! Didn't see that coming, did you!?

But think about it: Even if you don't *love* that skill you have, if you are good at it, then you probably get some pleasure from it, too. It simply feels good when you're able to do something well. You get a little dopamine hit from it.

Okay, perhaps it's not *that* chemically tangible, but you get the point: Doing something well can give you the juice to use that skill on a daily basis to build a side gig that eventually gives you the freedom to do *other* stuff you really like ... and that ultimately means spending time ***doing what you LOVE.***

ACTION STEPS

Take some time to answer these questions honestly:

- *What do I like? People ... or solitude?*

- *Do I like it quiet ... or noisy?*
- *Busy ... or technical?*
- *What am I good at?* List your skills and natural aptitudes. And then ask yourself: *Do I get pleasure from them?*
- Next, go to your list and score each one on the "Like" scale. Score them from 1 for "don't like" and 5 for "really like," and then score how often you'd be using that skill for that particular side gig.

Yes, this will take a little guesswork on your part. But try it!

When you're done, you should have some ideas that scored low enough to just delete them. For the ones that scored very high, it's time to focus on them and figure out which ones will be the best fit for you.

As you go through the process, your list will hopefully go from about 20 ideas down to 10 ... back up to 20 … and then, finally, down to three or four that rank the highest.

So the obvious question becomes: How do you choose from the remaining three or four at the top? That's largely personal, and also circumstantial.

Let's drill down:

If one of those ideas is something you can find and buy, then you go with that one.

If one of those ideas requires more work up front, but has a higher likelihood of producing passive income later, then that's a better choice than a gig that requires less time but may not have long-term passive income down the road.

As you can see, there is more to consider than just the items we've put into the Side Gig Calculator. But it remains a great tool to help you objectively compare and sort many side gig ideas so that you can narrow your search to just the best few.

Chapter 22

What's Your Side Gig?

I hope the various stories in this book have stimulated your brain. I also hope you took the exercises seriously, and began the process of brainstorming your own side gig ideas. If you'll remember, I suggested you read through all the stories before you start your own side gig. I also want you to finish this chapter, as well as the next. Why? Because in them we'll work through even more possibilities for your side gig. Then we'll discuss what you *shouldn't* do as a side gig. Finish reading these before you leap into something.

Let's talk through ways to plan your side gig.

Start With Your Strengths

Start by looking for the low-lying fruit of what you're already good at. You should never start a side gig (or a business, for that matter) without first focusing on what you already know how to do. I've written about this in my book *Do What You Love!* Unless you are already super rich, the most reliable way to climb out of poverty (or out of the rat race) is to focus on what you are already good at. Focus on your strengths. What does that mean? Consider your skills, knowledge, relationships, and any other various resources you may have at your disposal. Remember the exercises from Chapter 2? Take another look at them.

Your Skills

Your skills might revolve around what you do with your hands. My parents were skilled at woodworking, leaded glass work, and a number of other manually dexterous things. If those are your greatest skills, then don't try to become a web programmer. Look for side gigs that can be done with your existing skills.

In some cases, you may not need specialized skills. Remember my relative and his used book liquidation business? He needed to become a little computer savvy. But he relied on good software to make it happen. He needed to know how to use postal software to print labels and postage. But he didn't need an advanced education degree or specialized training.

Do you have any particular training, skills or aptitude? Then you should consider side gigs that exploit those skills. I've met warehouse managers who think they have no skills. They have a great skill, and many small companies would pay for consulting from someone with that type of expertise. You'll likely command a higher value for whatever you offer through your non-business if you focus on your existing skills. You want to maximize your value. You want to make the most you can for the least amount of your time. In addition, by doing something you are skilled at, you reduce your risk of making costly mistakes. You ensure the success of your non-business by doing what you are good at.

What Do You Know a Lot About?

While capitalizing on your skills is key, so is doing what you *know* really well. What is your knowledge base? You might know a subject really well, even though you are not really an expert. Your knowledge can still be an asset. I knew a physician whose skill was software coding. His first few years of medical practice were very low paying. He had a side gig developing software, even though it wasn't his profession. He was just doing something he had a lot of knowledge about.

If you want to make money from blogging or running an information website, you don't have to be the No. 1 expert. You just have to be knowledgeable. Content-based websites succeed because they have unique, original content that people find useful. If you enjoy a certain subject, you might be able to use that knowledge to create a fan site, a blog, or content site that brings revenue from ads, membership, or the sale of related products. Who knew that your closet affinity for 17th Century harp music had the potential to bring value? But it does! You could be the one who curates content around your chosen subject, and thus become the go-to information destination on the Web.

If you feel skill-less, knowledge-less and hopeless, stop it. I've already shown you that side gigs can arise from things that require little skill or knowledge. But you can also see that you'll have even greater opportunities for side gigs if you begin to add to your knowledge or skill base. Maybe your first side gig is just a stepping stone to the next. If that's the case, then get going on your first non-business, and at the same time commit to expanding your knowledge so that you have greater options down the road.

Who Do You Know?

They say life is about who you know, not what you know. This is not completely true. Life *is* actually about what you know. But who you know is still important. The people you know will also be an important factor when you contemplate a side gig. Consider my friend Jim's construction glue side gig described in Chapter 1. He needed his old network from his construction years to create a channel of buyers for his private label glue. If you want to manage property, then it helps if you know someone who owns property.

A word of warning, however: Be careful with your personal contacts. Don't treat them the way multi-level marketers do. Yes, your contacts are indeed your built-in "warm market." But they're also your friends, family and acquaintances. Treat them with respect and make them a collaborative part of your non-business, not merely the target of a product or service you want to sell. The golden rule is still the golden rule: treat others how you want to be treated.

What Resources Do You Have at Your Disposal?

What tools do you have already? If you are equipped with the resources to mow a lawn or build shelving, and if those things fit your skills, then those can be combined to create an effective non-business.

Do you have the equipment to work on car stereo systems? Use them. Maybe you have a skill in graphic design and a computer powerful enough to apply it. Use those resources.

Money is a big resource to consider. Some non-businesses can be started with very little cash. Others need $10,000 or even $20,000. I've bid on bankruptcy assets whose cost ran up to six figures. You can't make a side gig out of buying IP assets if you don't have the resources to buy them from bankruptcy. Carefully consider the capital requirement for your side gig. It should be low. But, of course, "low" has a different meaning to a dentist than to a retail store clerk.

A side gig can be started with just a few hundred dollars. You've also seen many examples in this book that require more than that. If your ideal side gig requires more cash than you have, then save and wait. Don't borrow or put it on a credit card. Your goal in having a side gig is to climb your way out of the rat race and achieve financial independence. To do that you need to own your side gig and not saddle yourself with debt. Business debt is sometimes necessary and reasonable. But not for your side gig.

Take stock of your resources: cash, income, tools, technology. Even your home. If you are going to use AirBnB to rent a room or a sofa, for example, then assess that asset honestly and be sure it matches the non-business you have in mind. A person will pay handsomely to crash on the sofa of a nice flat in Manhattan, but they might not ever want a room, even a luxurious one, in Duluth, Minnesota. The reason is that there are cheap hotels in Duluth, while a hotel in Manhattan starts at several hundred dollars per night.

ACTION STEPS

It's time to go back through your previous exercises. Start with Chapter 1, and move through all of the exercises. As you do, start highlighting the things that stick out. Cross out things that clearly strike you as business ideas that are inconsistent with what's been taught in this book.

Chapter 23

Ideas and Examples of Side Gigs

Redd Horrocks was an average resident of Las Vegas, Nevada. She was trying to make ends meet and manage her debt load. Redd once used the freelance service Fiverr for help in completing a small project. I've mentioned Fiverr before. As hard as it might seem, there are literally thousands of tasks people will do for just five bucks, and Fiverr is the platform for connecting those people with customers willing to pay. For example, you can have a photo turned into a cartoon image, or get a logo created, for just five bucks.

Redd tripped onto Fiverr as a customer, but then realized that she could offer a service herself. She had done voiceover work in the past and created an offer on Fiverr to do a 125-word voiceover for $5.00. She went from earning a few hundred dollars per month to over $1,000 per month. With a little better marketing, she hit $3,500 per month. Her goal was to use Fiverr to get out of personal debt. By 2015, she was making $9,000 to $11,000 per month, and not even working full-time. She got out of debt and ended up purchasing the house she was renting.

All it took for Redd was a new idea that came to her from seeing something she had never considered. Here was a platform that would let her leverage her talent and change her life forever. My goal in this book is to load you up with ideas you may have never considered, and then let you gravitate toward something that will become *your* life-changing side gig.

Throughout this book, I've given you a variety of ideas about side gigs. Many are the true stories of successful side gigs of other people, as well as my own. Along the way I've suggested various ideas related to these real world examples. In this chapter, I'd like you to consider some additional ideas that may lead you to a non-business that's right for you.

YouTube

There's just no other way to say it: People are making millions on YouTube for the most ridiculous things. How about a faceless person who opens Disney toys on camera? She makes millions (I'm not kidding; Google it). Or a guy who eats things like an entire can of Crisco or a tube of construction goop? Makes millions. The kid who simply films himself playing with games and the girl who videos herself shopping? Making millions. Now I'm not telling you to go copy these folks. But make no mistake: There is a massive money-making opportunity on YouTube for original content.

Think about it. Where do you go when you want to learn something? YouTube, right? A few years ago, I wanted to learn how to program in X Code. I was a total amateur and just wanted to get behind the veil to learn enough to speak intelligently about Apple programming, particularly mobile apps for Apple devices. What did I do? I watched a series of how-to videos taught by an 11-year-old kid on YouTube. I was able to follow along and recreate what he was showing on video. His videos had hundreds of thousands of views.

One of my hobbies is art. Again, I'm an amateur. But learning is so convenient and easier with YouTube. I recently watched a 10-minute lesson in drawing the human eye. It was a great lesson ... *that had over 11 million views*. After watching the lesson I pulled up an online calculator and concluded that the author had earned anywhere between $14,960 and $37,400 from YouTube's ad revenue sharing program. *For just that one video*. That same author has many other videos, too. Even if each video brought in just $3,000 per year, 10 such videos would net you $30,000 per year.

Consider your expertise and how you could present useful content. Cooking? I make a fantastic panna cotta. I could create a video showing how I do it, along with a dozen other recipes, each of which could create ongoing revenue for me that could last many years. What about you? Can you show people how to change their brake pads? Make a video. Can you shuck oysters better than most? Maybe you can create a channel where you read Harry Potter books in Klingon. Whatever your expertise, you can probably find a way to monetize it on YouTube.

YouTube is not the only source for showcasing your expertise. Let's look at more formal learning platforms.

Udemy Teaching

There are a dozen online learning sites, and several of them are enormous. One of the largest is called Udemy, boasting seven million students. It's known as a "massive online open college" or MOOC. These sites offer an opportunity for those with a particular skill or expertise to teach that skill in a video course. I happen to teach a course on Udemy. While my course is free, I can switch it to paid whenever I want. In addition, for the students who like my course (3,000 have viewed it so far), I could produce additional courses and expand my reach as well as my income.

I am also an author at LinkedIn Learning, the largest online video training site in the world. While Udemy allows anyone to teach, LinkedIn Learning engages authors directly. This means unless you are a noted expert in your field, it's much harder to get your content out through LinkedIn Learning. If you are a respected expert in your field, and have a solid ability to present that content in plain English, sites like LinkedIn Learning offer an attractive channel for teaching your subject.

Other platforms you can leverage for your content include Coursera, Udacity, EDX, Khan Academy, CreativeLive and Curious. But given the stream of revenue that people are making from YouTube, don't exclude that option either. In fact, if you are an expert in something, why not offer your content on *all* of these platforms?

The wonderful part is, video content is perennial. It will continue to produce income for many years, and you won't have to do anything else once you produce your course and upload it. What better side gig than one that requires no ongoing effort on your part? You don't need four hours per month for this side gig; you just focus enough energy at the beginning and then let it run and enjoy the long-term benefits.

Small Web Businesses

The list of side gigs you could operate on the Internet is too long to list here. Blogging can pay if you have something to say and can attract readers. Fan sites and content sites around niche content is still a great idea. Are you a Barbara Eden fan? You might be able to garner a large amount of traffic by running an "I Dream of Jeannie" blog. If you have some particular knowledge of a subject, even if it is a narrow niche, you might be able to start from scratch and make money from advertising revenue. Remember that informative ebook I purchased for $9.99 before moving to Bali? The same author runs a blog that makes money from ads, ebook sales and consulting. It's a small niche, but in a world of nearly eight billion people, appealing to a narrow niche is not only viable, it can actually be an advantage. When it comes to side gigs, small and narrow can be right where you want to be.

If you don't want to start from scratch, you can also scour sites like Flippa and Merger Network for web businesses that are for sale. In many instances you can find a site that someone has spent thousands of dollars on, or that a developer has spent hundreds of hours developing, and buy it for a few thousand dollars.

On the one hand, the opportunities are numerous. On the other hand, it's strictly buyer-beware. Be careful about buying something that is broken. In fact, the best deals *will* be broken somewhat. By "broken" I don't mean it's so broke you can't fix it! Think of buying a used car that needs a starter and not much else. Similarly, you can buy a web business whose missing or broken piece is something you can provide.

Maybe all it's missing is some attention! Give it some love, feed it, run it better and you might increase revenue substantially! If you choose to snap up a bargain website, be sure you are ready to invest some additional time and money in improving it.

Here are a few examples of current listings on Flippa:

Right now as I'm typing this, I see an auction for an established site with 25,364 unique visitors per month. It is making $528 per month and has 70,000 registered users. While there are 14 bidders currently, the price is still under $1,500 for the entire site. That would be recouped in three months or less.

Have a little more money to spend? Here's one that's under $10,000: Two busy Minecraft sites, making $1,769 per month. The only cost to operate these sites is the hosting ($40/mo), and your time.

How about a five-year-old site that sells patio furniture? It gets 1,785 views per month and brings in $610 per month on average. This site can be had for less than $2,000. Does this mean you would have to ship patio furniture? No. You simply forward the sale to another site that will do the fulfillment for you. You would just run the website and keep doing whatever the former owner has done.

These are just three examples of the kind of excellent opportunities you can find on Flippa after a little digging. If you work through the exercises I've prescribed in this book, you can do even better.

Sell Your Music

Are you a musician? Have you considered alternative ways to make money as a musician? One way is to stop looking for a recording label to sign you and seek other means of distribution. Think outside the box. Maybe your music can make money from licensing rather than waiting for consumers to find you. AdRev (http://cid.adrev.net/) lets you make money by allowing YouTube users to use your music and you receive a portion of the licensing fees.

There are also websites that license music on a royalty-free basis. They charge users a fixed fee to use music on their site. There is great demand for this, notably from all sorts of companies for commercial use. A hotel chain, for example, would much rather pay a reasonable license fee for a clip of music to use, say, in a television ad rather than paying a production company tens of thousands of dollars to create their own tracks with studio musicians.

Users of these sites pay a one-time fee without obligation to pay ongoing royalties. The model is much like iStockPhoto and Getty Images, which do the same thing for photos and video. This is simply another marketplace to sell your music, which means musicians now have an opportunity to not only create their own hands-free side gig, but perhaps establish their own launch pad to stardom. Electronica musician Moby, for example, was a relative unknown DJ and songwriter until he began licensing his work for use in commercials, films and TV programs. Those licensed songs helped vault his 1999 album "Play" to 12 million worldwide sales, the biggest selling album of its genre.

One site that lets you sell your music as "stock music" is SoundDotCom (http://soundotcom.com/sell). Another is SoundJungle (http://audiojungle.net). You can upload your music on music distribution websites like these and make ongoing royalties.

Obviously, as a musician you can perform your music and produce a video and make money from YouTube directly. You can also put your music on iTunes and other paid channels. You can promote yourself on Soundcloud to get your music "out there," and then look for opportunities to license your music. One artist I know makes royalties from a license to a video game maker, which also gives his music broader exposure.

Artists who hustle can make their music into a side gig. Of course, performing at local bars can add up to a decent monthly income as well. Bottom line, you don't have to get signed to a label to make a good side gig income as a musical artist.

Mow a Lawn, Clean a Pool (Start Small)

You've already been lawn mowered out with my examples in this book, right? But I'm not done yet! Side gigs like this are simply not to be dismissed. Look at ways to use your time that give you a far better value than what you currently get at your day job. At the time, I was making $8 per hour at my retail mall job and made $25 per hour mowing lawns. It was a good use of my time. My earlier example of the pool cleaning guy showed that one could work just four hours per month to earn $400. That's $100 per hour. If your labor is what you can sell, then sell it wisely. Cut hair. Run errands for someone. Clean chimneys. There are a thousand ways to use your time in a way that lets you earn more than a typical hourly job. Over time you will get better at how you price the jobs you perform, and you will improve your overall income-for-time ratio.

Offer a Service on Fiverr (Or Better Yet, Sell a Service That You Outsource to Someone on Fiverr)

I mentioned Fiverr earlier in this book, but this particular freelance platform bears repeating as its own category in this chapter. Why would I recommend a site where you get paid only five lousy bucks for all manner of tasks? Here's why: What you sell on Fiverr could be something that takes you minutes to accomplish, not hours.

What kind of things do people offer on Fiverr? Here are some examples of listings:

I will model holding a sign.

I will record anything you want as a horse race.

I will draw a vector cartoon of you.

I will write an awesome page about you.

I will edit a page you write.

I will speed-paint your logo and tagline.

I will do a 3D CAD model for you.

I will write your essay or research paper.

I will write a 600-word article on any subject.

I will fix a WordPress error or customize your theme.

I will send your music to 300 college radio stations.

There are literally thousands of tasks people will do for five bucks. Why? Because they know how to do it very efficiently.

If you can do the same thing over and over, and do five or six of them in an hour, then you will make $25 to $30 per hour. Better yet, many of the tasks on Fiverr start at $5 but easily become $20, $30 or $50 gigs with extras. Are you thinking what I'm thinking at this point? "Wait a second, Dana … what if I actually find customers who will pay me $20 or more for something, and then I have *someone else* do it for $5?"

Gold star for anyone who had that exact thought. And sure, why *not* look at what people are willing to do for $5 … and then find a niche in the same space but market yourself to do the work for *more* than five bucks?

You could even automate something, depending on how sophisticated you are with technology. For example, if you had a website where people pay you $10 through PayPal to create a vector cartoon of their face, you could automatically send that to someone who is willing to create it for $5. You then deliver the product and keep the $5 profit. You don't have to be a graphic artist who is skilled at taking photos and making cartoons out of them. You simply rely on someone else to do that while you focus on marketing.

Your Own Amazon Store

Maryanne has a successful business doing graphic design. But it is a real business. She has to deal with clients every day. She has an office and staff. She has to manage her time so that she makes enough to pay her bills. She can't just skip off and spend a month in Bali. However, she can swing this if she launches a side gig allowing her to generate income not tied to her time. And once that is generating enough income, she can slow down her graphic design business and spend more time traveling. That is exactly what Maryanne is doing. I met her in Bali, and she's building her side gig and scaling down her design company over time.

What is Maryanne's side gig? She buys handbags in Indonesia and sells them on an Amazon store. Here's what is unique about Amazon: Maryanne can ship many handbags to Amazon all at once and then let them handle fulfillment. Maryanne doesn't have to dropship a purse every day. That's important for a businesswoman who wants to travel. She would like to spend a month or longer going to different places in Indonesia, Thailand, and Latin America, traveling and hunting for beautiful, inexpensive purses. She then sends those to an Amazon warehouse to fulfill her customer orders.

I can't tell you Maryanne's profit because I don't know it. But I know someone else who buys jewelry in Bali for $3, and then resells the same piece for $20. If she sells to a retail store at wholesale, then she sells it for $13 to $16. Thus, a $3 ring can make her $27 in profit. That's 800% profit. Even at wholesale, she's making four to five times her cost!

The great thing about running an Amazon store is that you don't have to set up a website of your own. In my view, setting up a website is easy but remember, I watch 11-year-old kids teach lessons on programming iPhone apps for fun. I like building web sites. But many people hate the idea of setting up a website and don't want to spend the money to have someone else do it for them. They don't want to deal with the merchant processing or customer tracking. Amazon — perhaps the most trusted online merchant in the world — does all that for you. They'll even send you traffic. And you can open your own online retail store in a matter of minutes.

Some entrepreneurs take the Amazon store model to another level by importing bulk quantities of items from China. You could consider buying products on Alibaba.com that might sell well to the U.S. market. You could buy 1,000 units of something and then resell those on Amazon or eBay. Two caveats: First, if you can buy 1,000 units of something, then so can your neighbor. So choose wisely and understand your competition. Find something unique and do your best to specialize so that you have a competitive advantage. Second, don't assume that just because it is available for sale that it is legally safe to sell. I've had several clients learn this the hard way. In one case the client purchased iPhone cases that bore the brand of a well-known company. They were not, in fact, from that company. They were fakes. The factory had sold 1,000 units to my client without telling my client that these were not from, or authorized by, the actual brand. He ended up being sued for thousands of dollars. Stick with products that are less likely to be knock-offs, or branded improperly. There's money to be made in this business, but one must be cautious about the sale of name-brand products.

Amazon isn't the only place to host your own store. You can sell your own products on Etsy as well. You might do something like Eric, who from his own garage transformed glass bottles into beer glasses and vases. You can offer that type of product on Etsy, or even on Instagram. Remember the woman who shops at garage sales for small vintage decor? She buys only what she really loves. She then posts it to Instagram and lists a price. The first person to comment that they want the item becomes eligible to buy it. They consummate a PayPal transaction and the item is then mailed to the buyer. Pretty simple, right? And remember, Instagram isn't even an ecommerce platform. She's just using it that way because it works for her. She has a built-in market eager for what she might list next, and she has no competition.

Rent Your Garage

I've discussed this in earlier chapters. Your garage might be a valuable asset. Let's face it, most American garages are havens for consumer clutter, a repository of leftover impulse purchases just rotting away. First, consider your clutter and put it to work for you. Sell the old junk. Rent the old junk. Put it to use in your side gig. Once your garage is clear, consider what that space could be used for. Let someone rent the whole thing if there's value in doing so. In urban areas, that garage might command several hundred dollars every month.

It may seem unlikely, but you might be able to rent your garage to someone who wants to use it for storing instruments — or yes, even for band practice. Put an overhead storage system like HyLoft in your garage and make room for something else to use the space effectively. You could even just rent a little bit of garage space to a friend or relative and still use the rest of the garage for yourself.

AirBnB a Room

The idea of renting your sofa, room, or even an entire house, freaks out many people. If you just can't stand the idea of some stranger sleeping on your sofa, or using your bathroom, then skip this. But if you have a Fonzie Flat with its own separate entrance, then your renters would not be in your space or sleeping on your sofa. You wouldn't even have to see them. They would have their own access and their own bathroom. A Fonzie Flat could pay your mortgage with the income you make from short-term rentals.

As I discussed in previous chapters, you can carve out a separate space in your home, attic, garage — or even a motorhome on your property — and rent it out on a short or long-term basis. Short term requires more turnover, and more contact with renters. There's more work involved, but the income will be higher than what you would receive from a monthly renter.

If you are more adventurous, you can do as my friend does and rent your apartment for a weekend each month, and go crash at a friend's house.

Upwork Something You Do Well

Let's say you want to sell your time, but you don't want to get dirty like a landscaper. Can you sell your time in a more sanitary profession? Yes. How about selling something you do virtually? Sell a service that you provide over the Internet.

Like what? Well, if you look at Upwork (formerly Odesk and eLance), you'll see thousands of services that people offer for sale. Edit someone's ebook and make $500. Create a logo and make $200. Be a virtual assistant to some busy entrepreneur and make a few hundred dollars per month. Photography. Modeling. Graphics. Programming. Sales. Cold calling. I've used Odesk to have someone sort through large blocks of data, write computer scripts for analyzing that data, and even once had someone write a custom program to organize the data from an old legal dictionary so that I could post it on one of my websites. Look at what services others are offering and consider what you may want to do.

Upwork is not the only place to sell your services. Look at other sites such as TaskRabbit. The increased exposure will generate more revenue for you. Think of Upwork as the source for selling a virtual service, and TaskRabbit as a way to sell your physical presence. For example, help someone move, fix something for a sweet elderly person, go shopping for a busy working mom, or help run a party or event.

Cosulting

You don't have to only sell a service. You can actually sell your advice. You can provide consulting for a fee through a wide number of websites. For example, GrowtheGeeks lets you offer services such as posting social media for a small company. Plansify.com lets you offer your expertise to others who are traveling and want advice about locales they want to visit. There are many other sites geared toward letting you sell yourself as a paid consultant, both professional and personal. Maybe your side gig is being a life coach for a few hours per week. You'd get to help change people's lives while making money every month.

Sell an Ebook

If you are considering offering a consulting service (like you can with Plansify) or teaching people how to do something in a video course (like Udemy), then you should also consider making an ebook. Of course, you could create a standalone ebook and stop there. But if you are going to build a revenue-generating non-business around your expertise, then you should consider all three avenues: ebook, video courses, and consulting.

Before I took my sabbatical to Bali, I found an ebook online titled "The Bali Manual." I paid a reasonable price for it and learned a lot. But then I also paid the website owner for an hour of paid consulting to ask questions and learn even more. I got every dime's worth of value from that ebook and consultation. It was a very cheap way to learn invaluable information about a place I was about to travel to for the first time. It saved me a lot more than what the book and consulting cost.

Don't want to write an ebook? Outsource it to someone on Upwork! Give them the information you possess and have an expert writer help you put the ebook together. Do the same for your videos. You don't need to edit videos or put slides into your course. Let others do what they are good at.

Blog, Fansite, Affinity Site

I've already mentioned the idea of running your own blog, fansite, niche content site, or even a larger content site such as Freelegalaid.com. Curate awesome content and you'll eventually get traffic. Review books. Discuss whatever niche-y, controversial topic you may be passionate about, like UFOs or colloidal silver. Talk about your expertise in horticulture, cooking, woodwork, or underwater basket weaving. Build a content site around home remedies, freediving, bass fishing, or motorcycle repair. As long as you are building solid content that people find useful, you can build traffic. And once you have traffic, you'll have ad revenue.

Ad revenue is not the only way to make money from a website. You can create a membership site where members get premium content for a fee. You can also find a product to sell on your site that's related to your subject matter. My buddy John from Chapter 6 makes money on ads, but since his website has tools for editing photos, he also offers products such as photo-to-canvas, posters, and prints. This brings in extra money in addition to the ad revenue. Of course, if you happen to have an ebook or video course that's related to the subject of your site and would be of interest to your visitors, you can use the site to promote those as well.

Don't have your own products to sell? No problem. You can become an affiliate and sell someone else's product or service. Just remember that it needs to be related to the subject at hand. If you run a fansite, you can be a ticket sales affiliate and push fans to a ticket seller who will pay you a commission on ticket sales you refer. Affiliates can make as much as 50 percent on customer purchases. You don't have to sell anything. You just have to send the customer to the affiliate's site with your own customized link that does all the tracking for you. It's a true win-win: You're recommending something your website visitor already wants, and then you get to keep a chunk of the sale if they end up purchasing something from the vendor you've recommended.

These are just a handful of non-business ideas. If you use them to brainstorm more ideas, you'll come up with dozens more and perhaps hit upon the perfect non-business. Use these to spawn your own creativity and think outside the box.

Join a Gig Platform

I've already mentioned many of the platforms that allow you to earn side gig income through an existing website. What is a gig platform? It is a central website that allows buyers and sellers to find each other. I mentioned a few of these at the outset. Consider the vast number of gig platforms. AirBnB lets you rent your room, apartment or condo by matching you with potential renters. Uber and Lyft let you work as a freelance driver by matching you with consumers who need rides. Piggyback lets you do the same with packages rather than people. Luxe matches you to a valet to park your car when you can't figure out where to park in a big city like New York or San Francisco. BlaBlaCar lets you share your commute. Instacart lets you shop for someone who needs groceries bought and delivered. Drizzly does the same for booze. TaskRabbit lets you do the same with all sorts of tasks, including shopping. Fiverr lets you sell your gig to millions of potential buyers. Etsy lets you sell your handmade items to millions of customers. There are hundreds of platforms that are the "Uber of ____." There literally are hundreds of platforms that let you easily make money as a side gig.

These giant platforms offer an easy way for people like you to get started in the gig economy. These sites are not the only way to score a side gig — in this book I've provided many more examples of side gigs that are more independent and potentially lucrative — but the fact that these platforms are growing is an indication that Americans increasingly want to work on their *own* terms. This includes dictating how they work, when they work, and how much they get paid.

Whether you choose to find your own gig among the existing platforms, start your own, or acquire one that is already making money, your side gig should give you greater financial freedom and more control over your time and energy.

Chapter 24

What Not to Do for a Side Gig

One reason I asked you to read the entire book before you start your side gig is to steer you away from things that tend to do poorly as non-businesses. In fact, these also tend to be challenging as real businesses, too. Take a look at the following areas and consider staying away from them.

Apparel

It seems everyone wants to own an apparel line. But if you aren't a celebrity, or already in the fashion business, the barriers to entry are massive. I can't tell you the number of entrepreneurs I've worked with who've tried to launch an apparel brand and failed.

The most common mistake people make is that they think simply coming up a catchy name or great logo is enough. This is rarely the case. The USPTO trademark database is a boneyard for good apparel brands that never made it. If you can think of a cool-sounding name for an apparel brand, someone has probably already filed to register it, tried to launch … and failed. People rarely buy a brand simply because they like the name or the logo. People buy because the brand has established its presence in the fashion community. People buy brands because they like the style, the quality, and the price. Brands like FUBU or Zoo York succeeded because people wanted to be associated with a certain desired subculture that already existed. But unless you are Ashton Kutcher or Daymond John, you are not likely to establish a lifestyle brand that draws people to you as a symbol of your lifestyle or personality.

Moreover, apparel is a highly competitive business. Those who are successful have access to high quality manufacturing at low prices. They have worldwide distribution. They have licensees who pay advances and generate revenue in sub-markets and in dozens of other countries. Apparel isn't just the domain of the experienced entrepreneur, it's a lion's den for those experienced *specifically* in apparel.

Finally, apparel is rarely a non-business. Apparel is not an easy business to outsource and manage from your villa on the Mexican Riviera. If you want to create a side gig, it needs to be a non-business. Steer clear of apparel with very few exceptions.

Cosmetics, Lotions and Potions

I've had the unfortunate experience of seeing more than one entrepreneur dashed on the rocks of the cosmetics and lotion industry. I'm not sure what the draw is, but I've personally seen more than a few try and fail. They certainly would not have worked out as side gigs, either.

Cosmetics, lotions, soap, toiletries, and the like are all commodities. They are widely available to competitors who have massive infrastructure and economies of scale. A new entrepreneur should stay out of this space unless she was already an executive in the market.

High Capital Outlay Ideas

One of the reasons I've advised against going into apparel is because it is a "high capital" idea. But it is not the *only* high capital idea. Consider what it will cost to run your side gig and be sure you don't need to spend a lot up front, or invest much along the way.

I know of someone who started what he thought was a side gig by importing a container of teak furniture from Indonesia. It cost him $40,000. And it took him a year to slowly sell the furniture. He made a little money, but not the profit he expected. But he had to put $40,000 at risk at the very start. That's quite stressful. Some businesses require even more capital at risk. Franchises, for example, are high capital outlay businesses. While franchises can be a solid business, they are rarely a perfect side gig. They often require far too much capital to buy into, and then they require ongoing investments of your time.

Can a franchise work as a side gig? Yes, although it is rare. However, I *can* tell you one story about a franchise owner who didn't have to put in the intense, continual work that's usually standard fare for franchise owners. This man owned four franchises of the same fast food chain. At first he worked hard as the owner and manager. But within a few years he found and trained an amazing manager. This manager changed his life. The owner was able to move to another state, far away from his franchises. And by the time I met him, he had spent the previous ten years surfing every day, walking his dogs along the beach, and generally enjoying life living in a $2 million house in a high-end neighborhood. He placed a phone call every other day to his manager, whom he paid very well and treated like royalty, paying her well above the norm and never taking her for granted. The business made enough over the years to allow him to invest in income property, stock, and build up a nice savings. So yes, you can certainly make it big with a franchise, and even develop that franchise into a side gig. It is just not as common (or easy) as you might think.

Retail and Restaurant

I've had the privilege of owning a cafe. It was the perfect business to teach me a valuable lesson. The lesson? Don't ever own a cafe!

I say that in partial jest. Restaurants can be wildly successful businesses. I can think of more than a few clients and colleagues who have made millions in the restaurant business. But they are the exception, not the rule. It is hard to make money in the restaurant business. In addition, restaurants require a massive up-front investment. They also require constant attention by the owner. You have to work long days, and you have to love being at your restaurant. Restaurants violate *every* rule of the side gig.

In my cafe, I worked 12 to 16 hours a day, seven days a week. I managed payroll for a staff of employees who were not always the best, some of them even stealing from me. I once had to sell one of my extra cars to meet payroll because, as is common in the restaurant business, income fluctuates such that you often have to plow more money into the business.

Retail stores are very much like my cafe. They have a physical location that demands your constant attention. You have to pay rent, regardless of whether you sell anything that day. You generally need employees, which means managing people, paying them and, yes, sometimes those employees steal from you. You also need to be ready to infuse capital at any time to cover new inventory. Retail is not generally a good non-business. It requires too much of your time, too much up-front capital and too much ongoing capital.

Custom Manufactured Items

I've been involved in a number of ventures that dealt with goods manufactured in Asia. I once invested in a venture that sourced goods from Asia for U.S. customers. I've had several lengthy tours of China with visits to manufacturing towns, factories, and offices. I love China. It is an amazing place. The manufacturing capabilities are amazing there. And it may surprise you to know that in my experience, wages were fair and working environments were clean, nice, and safe. China is the new America in many ways. It is doing what America once did: manufacturing the world's supply of metal goods, appliances, furniture, clothing and more. Because China has the ability to do this for a fraction of the U.S. cost, it has effectively given most Americans a raise in lifestyle. You can buy your furniture, appliances and clothing at a fraction of what they "should" cost, and that means more discretionary income for you.

You may not like China's emergence and think everything should be made in America. But I'm one who believes that

America's value is not in its labor. Even when we make things in America, who actually does the work? Mostly first and second generation immigrants. The typical American-born kid does not want to weld metal shelving all day. In fact, they won't. The people who *will* do the work are those who've migrated here from elsewhere. So it's my view that whether something is made in America with immigrants, or made in China with their own laborers, America should be thankful for the people willing to do the things we don't want to do.

What America does well is no longer in the world of physical goods, but in the world of ideas. America's balance sheet is virtually all intellectual property. We generate ideas that not only make a difference here in the United States, but all over the world. We engineer the next technology. We design interfaces. We make fashion. We create entertainment. We create brands. We market.

From a very young age, we as Americans are exposed to the best things in the world. A 12-year-old American can probably create a better marketing campaign than an educated person in a country where television and internet are not ubiquitous. I know this because I've traveled all over the world and have seen how terrible marketing is in many countries. We, as Americans, have a knack for marketing and branding because we're fully immersed in it from a young age. We're brought up in an IP-intelligent environment. Our current — and future — workforce is one that will generate intellectual property, not physical goods. And this is a good thing. It is what we are good at. It is what brings value to the rest of the world, and that value is what keeps America strong economically.

But what if you have a great idea for a business or side gig that includes producing a physical good? Well, of course it's never been easier to have it made in China. In fact, as I have mentioned, you can find existing products from thousands of Chinese manufacturers on Alibaba.com, and not even have to engineer the product. You just have to brand it and sell it.

What if your product is totally new, and not yet being manufactured? Well, that can be a problem. The first problem is that manufacturing a custom product is going to take significant time, require a lot of up-front capital, plus an ongoing investment of your time and money. You have to pay for custom molds, pay for samples, and then order a minimum quantity of products. And you do all that at the risk of the product not even selling. That's a tough hill to climb for any side gig. Second, even if your product *can* make it as a side gig, you need to ask yourself whether you want your unique product made by a factory that could easily turn around and sell it themselves on their own Alibaba.com site. If you want to eliminate that risk you need to get a patent not only in the

United States but in China, too. This might be acceptable if you are building a real business, but you can see how it steepens the uphill climb for something like a side gig.

As you explore side gig ideas, don't get sidelined by trying to do something that has high barriers to entry, low margins, high risk, capital requirements, or is something that requires you to spend time in factories in China. Stay out of businesses that fail often and easily like apparel, restaurants, cosmetics, lotions, and manufacturing.

Chapter 25

Conclusion

Thank you for sticking with me to the end! I hope you have used the exercises and done your brainstorming. Maybe you already have a short list of ideas that might work for your side gig. That's perfect! Don't jump into one thing until you are sure it's the right one for you. But also, don't get afflicted by "paralysis of analysis." Side gigs should be low-cost, and it's okay to fail. Don't hold back. Don't wring your hands and overthink it. Do your homework and then give it a try.

Now it's time to take all this information to the next level. Work through the exercises and review everything you've written down. Start narrowing down and gather more information about each side gig that seems the most viable. In this chapter, I'll leave you with some final homework. My tool at sidegigcalculator.com is something you can use to work through your ideas and move some to the front burner, while knocking out others that are not right for you.

Work through the Side Gig Matrix, and be honest with your answers. Use this to help you evaluate what you'd like to select as your non-business.

How much will each cost to launch? What are the barriers? What are the risks? What is the reward for each? Do you know the industry? Do you have contacts that will give you a leg up? Is it within the range of what you can invest? Does it match your resources? Does it match your tolerance for risk? Start to ask these questions and use our tool to rank your ideas so that you can exclude ideas that don't give you the best chance to succeed.

Remember the requirements for a good side gig!

- Low capital outlay
- Low ongoing capital requirement
- Low time required (two hours per week on average)
- Steady income of $200 to $400 per month base with the potential of making more without much extra effort
- Low liability, low risk
- Low stress

And remember these keys to success in any business:

- Do something you're good at, which will be something you like but don't necessarily *love*.
- Leverage your network (and continue to build your network).

- Drop big fancy ideas in favor of basic pedestrian ideas, where a stable market already exists.
- Build side gigs that give you more value for your time than you'd get by selling your time.
- Deploy your cash wisely.
- Build a side gig you can sell down the road, or one that might blossom into a full-blown business over time.

Made in the USA
Monee, IL
04 November 2026

67384436R10154